A New Phoebe

Perspectives on Roman Catholic Women and the Permanent Diaconate

Edited by
Virginia Kaib Ratigan
Arlene Anderson Swidler

Sheed & Ward

Sheed & Ward™ is a service of the National Catholic Reporter Publishing
Company, Inc.

Library of Congress Catalog Card Number: 90-60898

ISBN: 1-55612-357-4

Published by: Sheed & Ward
              115 E. Armour Blvd.
              P.O. Box 419492
              Kansas City, MO 64141

To order, call: (800) 333-7373

Contents

IV. Some Historical Background

Acknowledgements

This book may be considered a communal project involving input from many sources. We would like to thank Rosemont College President Dr. Dorothy Brown, and Academic Dean Dr. Anna-Maria Moggio, who offered generous support services; Margaret Loftus for her competent secretarial help; Dr. Robert Siegfried, head of the Graduate Program in Computer Education, for his guidance, along with graduate student Ginger Perrin, both of whom worked on the coding process for the questionnaire; Elizabeth Haskell and Sandi Clement for typing the manuscript; and Richard H. Strickler, Jr. for his help with the word processing.

At Villanova University, Father Francis Eigo, O.S.A., of the Religious Studies Department and the department staff were all helpful and encouraging in the task of sending out the questionnaires. Dr. John Kelley, Associate Director of the Human Organization Science Institute, generously shared his expertise in the formulation of the questionnaire.

Maureen McGovern provided valuable advice on wording the questionnaire from her perspective as a deacon's wife. The Sister Thea Bowman Foundation put us in contact with Mary Shelly, who gave us insight into her experience as a deacon's wife in the Black Catholic Community.

Besides the authors in this volume, many other people helped us to find women and men who were interested in this question. Margret Morche, Heinz-Willi Kehren and Jutta Flatters in Germany and Beth Gorman in this country were especially helpful. Sister Teresa Ahern, M.S.B.T., allowed us to call on her several times for assistance.

Early on in our project, Samuel M. Taub, then Executive Director of the Bishops' Committee on the Permanent Diaconate, shared his knowledge and helpful materials on the subject. Later his successor, Constantino Ferriola, updated statistics and other resources while giving encouragement during the final stages of our work.

Deacon Ademí Pereire de Abreu's interest in the question was discovered by Leonard Swidler, and the translation of de Abreu's essay from the Portuguese was provided by Philip Berryman. The comments of Sister Joaquina Carrion, M.S.B.T., were translated from the Spanish by Sister

Teresa Ahern. The three translations from the German were made by Ar-lene Swidler.

We would like to thank our families and interested colleagues for their suggestions and for proofreading.

Finally, our project was funded in part by a grant from the Pew Memorial Trust.

I commend to you our sister Phoebe,
a deacon of the Church in Cenchreae.
—Romans, 16:1

1

As We See It

Virginia Kaib Ratigan
Arlene Anderson Swidler

As an old proverb says, what one sees depends on where one is standing. This first section of the book is an overview of the situation of women and the permanent diaconate as we see it now. Our work emerges out of a shared experience that includes our own study of women and ministry, our teaching of courses on women and religion, and our involvement in the Catholic women's movement within the broader women's movement. We have felt the pain of Catholic women who have responded to the needs of others and who have sought to educate themselves in ministry. More and more women have worked for their Master of Divinity degrees; in years past, some were not even allowed to lector in their own parishes. Many wives of permanent deacons have been through the entire training program and have questioned the possibility of a call for themselves to this ministry in the Church.

It is with keen awareness that we witness the great drain of gifts and talents from the Roman Catholic Church as women are crossing over to other denominations in their spiritual journeys. They are ordained to diaconate and priestly ministry. Of course these gifts and talents are still present to us in the larger Christian Church, but we are left continuing the struggle for equality in the Roman Catholic Church with a diminishing pool of women. One woman we know has frequently described her condition as she continues to press for change: "I feel like a raisin on the living vine." Another woman who responded to our questionnaire to the wives of permanent deacons (discussed in a later chapter) stated that because of the lack of progress for women in the church she, and possibly her deacon husband, "may very well decide to worship elsewhere."

But why, we ask ourselves, have we chosen to focus on the diaconate for women? The question has been before us for a number of years. In those first years of renewal after Vatican II, Virginia Ratigan was conducting both college theology classes at Wheeling College and adult education programs in rural areas of West Virginia where women were already asking, "What is our role in all of this?" In 1970, when Arlene Swidler was working in the Washington office of the National Council of Catholic Women, she discussed the issue of women deacons with Father William Philbin, then the executive director of the Bishops' Committee on the Permanent Diaconate.

Why does it seem important now? Perhaps we are spurred on by the fact that from the re-introduction of the permanent diaconate in the post-Vatican II era there has been a continuous thread of support for the ordination of women to the diaconate. It has been on the American Bishops' agenda for twenty years, as Deacon Samuel Taub points out. However, there has been a continuous thread of opposition to the idea as well. These conflicting views have led us to examine the issue from a variety of perspectives, placing the permanent diaconate both in its present context and its historical setting. It has not been our intention to use what we discovered to prove a thesis about women and the permanent diaconate. We chose this format as an open forum for various participants to speak to the issue. If a worldwide meeting were called on the topic, these people with their array of backgrounds and experiences would all be competent speakers. Our materials are presented here to provide a basis for further dialogue on the issue, rather than to offer a single answer to the question.

As we participated in the years of preparation for the National Bishops' pastoral on the concerns of women, *Partners in the Mystery of Redemption*, we became ever more aware of the injustices and the conflicting opinions on the strategies for change. The permanent diaconate for women was a question that did arise in discussions. As it stands, the first draft of the document reveals a clear call for "thorough investigation" of the issue. The bishops go on to say: "We urge, therefore, that this study be undertaken and brought to completion soon. Women serving in pastoral ministry accomplish, by virtue of some other title or commission, many of the functions performed by ordained deacons and are capable of accomplishing all of them. The question of women being formally installed in the permanent diaconate arises quite naturally, and pastoral reasons prompt its evaluation."

We have no guarantee that this positive statement made in the first draft of the pastoral will remain in the final draft. In the end, will the U.S. Bishops finally support this investigation? Certainly individual bishops do. Bishop Howard J. Hubbard, of Albany, New York, has said that he strongly favors having women deacons and female acolytes in the Church. In an April, 1989, interview in the Kansas City-St. Joseph *Catholic Key,* the Bishop said that he was "positive" about the possibility of ordaining women deacons. He said that he wished the Vatican as more responsive to the issue of girl altar servers, and added that girls function as altar servers in the Albany Diocese despite the Vatican's opposition. The October issue of *St. Anthony Messenger* features an interview with Bishop Joseph L. Imesch, chairperson of the Bishops' committee drafting the pastoral. He predicts that the thorough study of the permanent diaconate for women will continue. On the issue of women acolytes, Bishop Imesch says, "I would certainly push that very strongly because in this area, at least to my understanding, there is no theological reason preventing women from serving. The issue has been floating around so long that it's become a nonissue. There is no country in the world where girls are not serving Mass."

Virginia Ratigan's essay on deacons' wives is based on the experience of those who are among the closest to the permanent diaconate as it is lived out today. This provides a very different basis for dialogue on this issue. Although many articles have been written by and about deacons' wives and the deacon couple, very little has been done to link these experiences to the larger questions concerning women and the permanent diaconate. Again, there has been some discussion about whether or not the diaconate for women is a good idea, but as yet little has been heard from these wives who, because of their own experience and formation, might seek this ordination if the structure of the institution were to change. There are, of course, many deacons' wives who already feel they participate intimately in the diaconate and would not necessarily seek it for themselves. In her 1987 autobiography, *Ministry and the Family of the Permanent Deacon* (The Liturgical Press, 1987), Dottie Mraz writes, "Once a woman has shared in her husband's ordination, she will always share in it . . . . Many deacons' widows will continue in the service their husbands were ordained to perform." Maureen McGovern says in her essay, "I share in the Order of Deacon by virtue of the fact that it was conferred upon my husband." Mary Shelly does "not aspire to be a deacon. My 'call' as a deacon's wife is a ministry and just as spiritual." On the other hand, John Williams, from his experience on the faculty of a diaconal formation program, sees a definite advantage when both husband and wife are ordained to the diaconate. "I can think of at least seven who could work better as a ministerial team than they are able to under the present solo arrangement."

Continuing the experiential and practical perspectives, there are several essays included in this book which are autobiographical. Catherine Stewart-Roache speaks for herself and other women in her New Mexican diocese who were—or are—ready and waiting for their ordination to the permanent diaconate. Barbara Sequeira describes her context and the feeling of being drawn to the diaconate as a result of her parish experience. Joanne Sullivan, S.H.C.J., shows her work in campus ministry leading her to a realization of her call to serve the needs of the college community by way of the permanent diaconate. A narrative of Catholic women's work toward the diaconate in the Minneapolis-St. Paul Archdiocese is included here as well; an Archdiocesan Commission on Women has been preparing a statement for a number of years. Without this input from everyday experience, the question of whether or not to open the permanent diaconate for women remains theoretical. Unless our discussions on the issue are rooted in the reality of life in the Church with all its diversity of perceptions, our dialogue on the diaconate for women will lack credibility.

Although this book focuses on the present, where for some years diaconal work for women has been arising quite naturally, as the Pastoral says, we want to set this activity in its historical context as well. Using the methodology of liberation theology, we have allowed the present experience to speak for itself before relating that experience to past history in our background essays. In both our research and teaching since the 1960s, we have studied feminist biblical scholarship and the ongoing work of reconstructing women's role in the history of the Church. Doing the historical background comes very naturally to feminists who have long searched for evidence of their foremothers' lives and work, sometimes in an effort simply to get to know them, sometimes to discover the links for moving on in their own time. One is aware of the limitations of the historical perspective when, as seen in Arlene Swidler's overview of the diaconate and women, her only available sources for the early periods are reports of males and laws. As this history is carefully reconstructed, one wonders if it will be possible to join the past history with present experience and witness a new Phoebe in contemporary Church life.

Not everyone is pleased with the idea of the diaconate, even for men. From the beginning a minority of Catholics, including a few priests, pointed out that the introduction of the permanent diaconate, clearly a result of the shortage of priests, allowed the Church to use married men in auxiliary positions and thus not confront the real issue—mandatory celibacy. These new deacons, they argued, would unwittingly be helping to maintain an outmoded status quo.

But most opposition is less theoretical and aimed more at the style the diaconate has taken or even at the deacons themselves. Usually the criticism revolves around what is seen as clericalism in the deacons. Father Richard McBrien of Notre Dame, for example, has said, "There are too many men who become deacons out of strong personal motivation rather than a response to demonstrated pastoral needs. There are too many of those types of deacons who have become more clericalized than the very priests with whom they serve." Or as William M. Droel put it in a 1984 article in *America,* "A significant number of deacons seem more comfortable dressed in albs than in leadership roles in the community."

Msgr. Ernest J. Fiedler, for many years executive director of the Bishops' Committee on the Permanent Diaconate in Washington, addressed this problem forthrightly in a 1986 article, "Permanent Deacons Shouldn't Play Priest," in *U.S. Catholic.* "There are too many liturgical deacons," he wrote. "I am not in favor of purely liturgical deacons acting like disappointed or mistreated second-rate priests." For many people, the Roman collar is the symbol of clericalism. "A deacon should not wear a

Roman collar," said Msgr. Fiedler. "Deacons wedded to the collar as a security are worse than Linus wedded to his blanket."

The readers polled by the magazine seemed to agree. Responding to the statement "When I see a permanent deacon wearing a Roman collar, I think he's trying to look like a priest," 55% agreed and 22% disagreed. And to the statement "A deacon is as much an ordained minister as a priest and therefore should be able to wear a Roman collar if he chooses," 20% agreed and 72% disagreed. A few of the responses enlarged on the topic. "In general the church is over-clericalized, over-ritualized, and under-evangelized," wrote one reader from California. "Unfortunately deacons fit into this mold along with the rest of us. Our deacons in this area are super-altar boys, mini-priests."

Another opposing view is directed more at practice than style. One respondent to our questionnaire noted that in her area of the country many deacons are not being given the opportunity to use their faculties, and much dissension and unhappiness results. Along the same line, another suggested that "a good many priests do not use or do not want to use the deacons as they should be used. . . . My observation is that they are threatened by them." And yet another felt that the priests and religious in her area were ignorant of the "deacon's role." A certain frustration shows in the remark of one respondent: "We have served three priests. None of the three welcomed the male deacon. I feel our priests need educating to help make the diaconate a success—male or female." The same theme is evident in this comment: "I feel at this time in our diocese men who are deacons are not totally accepted by the priests or the people. . . . People of our parish have mocked and made fun of my husband by referring to him as 'the bishop' or saying, 'who does he think he is' or totally ignoring him. I feel women deacons would be rejected in our parish at the present time."

When discussing the question of the permanent diaconate for women in Canada, our contact person, Catherine Berry Stidsen, noted that the lack of interest there might be due to the perceptions of the work of permanent deacons in the Church. There are several permanent deacons in the Toronto diocese; some people object to their "standing around like glorified altar boys. . . . A few serve as chaplains in Catholic high schools to support themselves and their wives; a few are high school teachers and are involved in the diaconate on weekends."

A more positive view can be found in the results of a 1988 survey in the Joliet Diocese. Rev. John Barrett of St. Alexander Church solicited the perceptions of priests, deacons and laity on the question of the diaconate and its level of acceptance in the Joliet Diocese. This evaluation tool showed clearly that the level of acceptance of the permanent deacons in most of their roles is very high (around 75%) after several years of their service in the parishes. Also the results indicated that the approval of these deacons went up the longer the deacons functioned in their parishes. The survey of deacons' own perceptions showed that they felt more accepted by pastors and laity than by parish associates and the diocesan priests. But they felt positive, on the whole, about their diaconal role. The laity surveyed were generally pleased with the integration of deacons into parish life.

Individual personal experience testified to the same thing. Sister Joaquina Carrion, M.S.B.T., currently Director of Diocesan Hispanic Ministries for the Diocese of Cleveland, has observed that through her contact with deacons "and with those who minister with deacons, I have witnessed their dependability, responsibility, integrity, and stability. They have made a permanent commitment to the ministry of the Church and feel personally responsible to carry out this commitment in their parish communities." She notes that "one area in which deacons have been especially helpful is in marriage preparation and marital counseling." A woman responding to our questionnaire to the wives of permanent deacons said, "My husband's experience as a permanent deacon has been a most positive one. As a high school principal, he brings many people-skills to the ministry. The most successful aspect of his role as deacon has been in his authorization to give homilies to the parish on a monthly basis. As the father of a teenage daughter and a young son, he has been able to communicate with the parents of the parish in a way the priest could never do. The people of our parish are most accepting and very supportive of his role in our church. Recognizing this approval, the priest too is supportive."

It comes as a surprise to many people that some of the strongest opposition to women in the diaconate comes from feminists. A good number of men, including theologians, priests and bishops, have been disappointed to discover that the female diaconate which they championed, sometimes against the majority of voices in the Church, was disparaged and rejected by many feminists. The disappointment is noticeable in the "Interview with Bishop Ernest Unterkoefler" included in this volume. That the feminist arguments against the diaconate differ and even contradict one another is to be expected in a broad movement where people are agreed on the goal—women's equality—but have varying ways of defining that goal or setting up strategies. There are several main arguments which we think should be considered.

The first is that women ought to be fighting against the clericalism which prevails in the Catholic Church and prevents it from being an institution responsive to the people. This has been very much a concern in the case of Episcopal women in the U.S. asking to be admitted to orders. Many women who felt that equality was an important goal have been reluctant to be brought into the clerical system. The Rev. Mary Anne Dorner, of St. Martin's Episcopal Church in Radnor, Pennsylvania, has noted that she and others feel a certain pull when theologically the emphasis is on lay ministry and declericalization and yet they are seeking admission to the clergy.

In 1983 the Women's Ordination Conference (WOC) took up the issue of women in the diaconate. The membership was divided on the advantages of pushing for the admission of women, and *New Women, New Church,* WOC's publication, printed articles and encouraged reader response on the question. Some of the negative arguments were summarized by Mary Hunt, including this argument that women should be thinking in terms of structural reform, of breaking the "link between those who minister and those who exercise decision-making." "For women to petition for membership in the clerical caste," she wrote, "with even the best of intentions of reforming it from within, seems to be a step away from the substantive structural reforms we seek." Objections of this sort parallel the arguments cited earlier which reject the permanent diaconate in general—for men as well as women. And some of them could be applied to the priesthood as well.

On the other hand, the international WOC conference in Baltimore in 1978, attended by more than two thousand people, had recommended that both the office of preaching and the Permanent Diaconate be opened to women.

The second argument is that women shouldn't settle for half-way measures. "No Mini-Ministries" read one pin popular with members of the U.S. Section of St. Joan's Alliance. Why not go all the way to the priesthood? If women are given the diaconate, it will just be a stop gap to keep them from thinking in bigger terms. They will still be inferiors in the Church. To accept the diaconate would be demeaning. The diaconate is second-class.

The third argument takes a somewhat different tack. Here too the emphasis is on the priesthood, but these feminists are worried that allowing women into the diaconate will actually lessen the possibilities of moving into the priesthood, once that is opened to them. One fear, fortunately, is not justified; a very small number of men have left the "permanent" diaconate for the priesthood after their wives died, and women would certainly be allowed to shift if the rules changed. But the main argument here is that the impetus for the priesthood would be drained away: women would feel content in the permanent diaconate and we could expect a long, long wait before Rome was pressured into taking still another step. The recent history of the Anglican Church in England and Australia, where women are still not ordained to the priesthood, has demonstrated that the diaconate alone for women has not been sufficient. Their recent "Presence" at the Lambeth Conference clearly shows their discontent with the lack of a transitional diaconate. There they were joined by their priested sisters from other parts of the world who had come to lend support and encouragement. The Rev. Suzanne Hiatt of the Episcopal Divinity School in Boston told us that "there has been a significant number of women coming to the U.S. from England to continue their studies for the priesthood."

Those of us who have been reading, thinking and talking about a women's diaconate for years are aware that there are still two ways of looking at the permanent diaconate, and that most of us view it from the two perspectives at different times. On the one hand, we see the permanent diaconate as a different sort of ministry from the priesthood with different tasks and different, not lesser, gifts. Women would seek the diaconate because it would incorporate their own gifts or would validate the ministries they are already performing. On the other hand, some see the admission of women to the permanent diaconate as one more step down the long road to full ministry and responsibility in the Church. Some of the essays in this book reflect that double vision. Representative of the first point of view is a response to a 1988 article that Arlene Swidler had written on the diaconate for women in *U.S. Catholic*. One woman said, "I act as a eucharistic minister in my parish. To be a deacon would help in making my ministry more authentic and visible in the eyes of the parish: taking Communion to the sick, lectoring, and leading two Scripture groups. Who needs status, you ask? It might do much to convert parishioners who are not quite ready to face the shortage of priests." A questionnaire respondent conveyed similar feelings, "I have been a pastoral associate on the pastoral team at a Geriatric Center for ten years and a full-time volunteer in the job for five years (20 hours a week). I do everything a deacon does (but never wear an alb) . . . . I have constantly upgraded my education by seminars and workshops."

It is clear in the essay of Joanne Sullivan, S.H.C.J., that her perceived call to the diaconate arises out of her campus ministry experience. Those she ministers to recognize her gifts and simply say: "You can do this work." Several responses in our questionnaire mentioned this validation of ministry. Some women felt that their involvement in retreat work, counseling, baptismal preparation and preaching is diaconal work which is simply not officially recognized. Wrote one woman: "I personally support and look forward to seeing women ordained in the permanent diaconate. (After all, women were deacons in the early church!) I believe the people in the parish will appreciate the unique vision women can give to the church just as married men have given through the diaconal ministry." Another woman wrote: "Since my husband's ordination. . .I saw a definite need in parish life for women deacons attached to a particular community and called to serve God's people in very unique ways. . . .There is much work to be done. . . .I have come to see ordained women especially suited to counseling ministries and family life ministries." In her essay "On Pushing for the Diaconate for Women," Irene Löffler-Mayer is taken by the irony of finding so many women in hospital pastoral ministry who, nevertheless, "cannot dispense the sacraments of the dying," as the situation demands. Across the border in East Germany, there is a tremendous shortage of priests, as Dr. Jens Langer, a theologian of ecumenics at the University of Rostock, has told us. Because of the pressing needs in his country, there are "a number of Roman Catholic women who would welcome a permanent diaconate for women."

Many women have seen so clear a distinction between the diaconate and the priesthood that they are opposed to the latter while favoring the former. The National Council of Catholic Women, for example, spoke positively on the diaconate for women in their 1979 "Position Paper on Women in the Church," while accepting the *Vatican Declaration's* rejection of women priests. "NCCW wishes to work together with other women of the Church in seeking to open wider ministries for women. We support the proposal to examine the feasibility of establishing the diaconate for women, a question the *Declaration* left open."

It is interesting that even some of the women who have written most strongly in favor of a revived diaconate or ecclesial ministry for women have themselves been opposed to, or at least unenthusiastic about, the priesthood for women. Kyriaki Karidoyanes FitzGerald, a leading Orthodox woman theologian, has written an essay on deaconesses. "As the example of the saints so clearly demonstrates, our Orthodox tradition bears a viable and valuable witness to the world of the many ways in which women have served the Lord and his Church. The order of the deaconess has been an important and significant one. And could not the Church in certain places benefit once again from this ministry of love and service?" Yet elsewhere she has spoken strongly against the priesthood. "Even to discuss woman's lack of participation in the ordained priesthood as an 'exclusion' implies that she can be 'included.' Woman is simply not called."

And Sister Mary Lawrence (Margaret) McKenna, S.C.M.M., whose 1967 book on *Women of the Church* is still an excellent sourcebook, said there, "Women need real representation in the visible Body of Christ. Regrettably, some few women feel that no other structure than the priesthood can provide that representation, so thoroughly clericalized has the

Church become in our day. The revival of permanent ministerial orders would be a step toward its needed de-clericalization."

Men too, of course, often draw the distinction between the call to the diaconate and the call to the priesthood. During the Second Vatican Council, Cardinal Richaud of Bordeaux said, "I have the impression that some priests have a vocation to the diaconate rather than the priesthood. The diaconate would have the advantage of bringing out the true nature of the priesthood as such."

On the other hand, there are certainly women who really feel called to the Roman Catholic priesthood, but would settle for the diaconate. For some, the permanent diaconate would be valuable primarily as a foot in the ecclesiastical door. Some might even hope to move on or up to the priesthood themselves. Others might rethink their call to the diaconate if the priesthood became a possibility. A look at the Protestant churches is useful here. Sophie Damme wrote in the Fall 1982 issue of *Liturgy*, "The number of deaconesses decreased after the opening of ordination to women, and again after the service of men and women in lay professions in the church gained greater recognition."

"The move from one form of service to another is not always a matter of immediate preference," however, as the Reverend Bertha T. von Craigh of the Evangelical Lutheran Church in America told us. "Sometimes the change or call of God surprises us in what we think is our intent to serve." In 1961, Pastor von Craigh believed herself called to serve the Church as a full-time career. By 1970, after completion of studies including a master's degree and internship in Christian Education and Youth Work, she became a deaconess and served in congregations. Consecration as a deaconess in the then-Lutheran Church in America was defined as someone who assists pastors, usually in congregational or institutional settings. It was only when she found herself in a position where she was in effect fulfilling many pastoral responsibilities and people were urging her to become ordained that she recognized a call to the ordained ministry. Prior to that, she says, "Ordination to Word and Sacrament had not been on my agenda."

The big question is whether, just as the transitional diaconate is a step toward the priesthood for individual men, the permanent diaconate for women can be seen as a step toward the priesthood for all women. Or would it prove a drawback? Bishop Imesch discusses this in the *St. Anthony Messenger* interview mentioned previously. He was asked whether some women might see the diaconate as a step toward achieving the ordination to the priesthood. He replied: "I think some might, although I must confess from our experience with permanent deacons that there has been no push on their part to be ordained to the priesthood. So I don't know if the one necessarily leads to the other." When asked how important the question really is, "We get it both ways," he replied. "We hear from women who are telling us that they will not accept the diaconate as a lure to get them away from the ordination to priesthood. And we hear others who say: 'This is very important for us. We would like to be able to preach—which is part of the deacon's role.' "

Here we all have to make our own judgments.

The 1971 *Guidelines* for the introduction of the permanent diaconate in this country made a relevant comment:

> The emergence both of extraordinary ministers and of pastoral teams will particularly affect people's attitudes towards women in pastoral ministry and even towards the ordination of women. Already people are beginning to see women distributing Holy Communion and exercising ministries of community leadership and personal counseling, in addition to the more traditional roles of teaching and visiting the sick. Aside from theological considerations regarding the ordination of women and from the evident need of apostolic workers, there is the vast pastoral dimension that considers people's attitudes, habits, and readiness to accept change.

Both of us have taught courses on women and religion for many years. We have taken our students on trips to observe Protestant or Jewish women officiating at worship, and we have seen how the experience has confirmed the students' conviction that ordination for women is the proper thing. Seeing women deacons in action, we think, would make a difference. Here, too, the experience of other churches is worth looking at. The Rev. Mary Anne Dorner is in the transitional diaconate at this time and will be ordained to the Episcopal priesthood within a year. She comments that "through the service of the woman deacon the community gets accustomed to women clergy. Because needs are being met, the woman issue is minimized."

From the beginning, deacons have been appointed to fill the perceived needs in the Church and world around them. As these needs changed, so did the role of the deacons. In the early Church, deaconesses had many tasks, but assisting in the baptism of women was the most important. As adult baptisms decreased, so did the number of deaconesses. Much later, the order of deaconesses was revived within Protestant churches, again to fill the special needs for ministry to women of that day.

Within Roman Catholicism, too, the permanent diaconate was reinstituted—for men only, of course—to meet the needs of the day. The first impetus came from Germany, where the experience of living as victims of the Nazi regime forced Catholics to rethink many aspects of Church life and structure they had earlier taken for granted. A Jesuit, Father Otto Pies, has written of the experiences of life in one of the three "priest blocks" in the concentration camp at Dachau in Bavaria; well over 2,000 priests and something like 60 Protestant ministers spent time there. Everything, he said, was concentrated in these concentration camps: misery, religion, pastoral care. Masks and disguises fell away as the men talked about the priesthood, about priestly formation, about priestly spirituality. And they wondered whether "this might not be the time to seize upon these impulses, which seem to be prompted by the Holy Spirit, that we place lay catechists and lay deacons at the side of priests? It would be easy to lay out the advantages which such a diaconate of married, employed and tested helpers would bring to the Church. And it would likewise not be difficult to draw the borders between the diaconate and the priesthood. The hierarchical church would sacrifice little and gain much."

During this same period, an official active in his Catholic parish was moved by the Nazis to a Protestant part of Germany to weaken his influence in the church. But in this diaspora situation, Josef Hornef discovered that he became even more involved in the life of the church, as the laity had to take over many of the duties of the priest, who came to town only once a week, and thus they took an active part in the liturgy, which would otherwise have been impossible. He began to see the value of a revived diaconate in a church of isolated Catholics, and when he came across Father Pies' article in the *Stimmen der Zeit* of October 1947, he felt moved to action. He began to write on the subject and soon became a leading proponent of the need for the diaconate.

West Germany continues to be a leader in the number of permanent deacons. In 1989 it had 1,342 men in the diaconate, second to the United States with 8,719, and far beyond any other country. The International Centre for the Diaconate (IDZ), directed by Margret Morche, is located in Freiburg im Breisgau. From its beginning in 1969, it has pursued the issue of women in the diaconate. Both Ilse Schüllner and Rita Gäng, who have contributed essays to this book, have published earlier articles devoted to the question of women and the diaconate in a special issue of *Diaconia XP,* published by the IDZ. Deacon Constantino Ferriola, National Director of the Permanent Diaconate program in the U.S., attended the April 1989 International Diaconate Conference in Fribourg, Switzerland, where he noted the wide support for women's ordination to the diaconate among the participants from around the world, especially among the Europeans.

When the question of a permanent diaconate was raised at the Second Vatican Council, the support from Latin America was surprisingly strong. Juan Cardinal Landazuri-Ricketts of Lima, Peru, speaking for 95 Latin American bishops, favored married deacons. Bishop Manuel Talamas Camandari of Ciudad Juarez, Mexico, speaking for eight Latin American bishops, told how deacons would lessen the number of civil marriages, minister to the dying and teach. The most famous intervention came from Bishop Jorge Kemerer of Posadas, Argentina. Speaking for 25 Latin American bishops, he pleaded for all the faithful left without a priest: "Do not take away our hope! The schema opens the door for the diaconate. We do not require you to go through it, but let those who wish to do so enter."

The report of Deacon Ademí Pereire de Abreu from Brazil, "A Brazilian View," emphasizes this argument on the basis of need. The diaconate for women is viewed as extremely important from the pastoral perspective. It is hard to imagine that in one diocese in Brazil alone there are a thousand communities without even a deacon. When faced with these statistics, discussing gender appears to be a luxury that the Church can scarcely afford. And yet Deacon de Abreu tells of his conversations with some priests and bishops who feel that since women are already doing diaconal work, this is enough. He points out the inherent injustice of such a view.

This exclusion of ministering women from the diaconate solely on the basis of sex creates deep pain. Lisa Bellecci-St. Romain of Baton Rouge, Louisianna, had discovered that two men who had worked with her in parish programs were going to be ordained to the diaconate. She told us of her bitterness at her "rejection" and her subsequent healing. "My husband and I have decided to cut our financial giving in half—25% to be restored when girls can serve at the altar and 25% again when women can be ordained."

The need for women in ministry today has been stressed by Bishop Mar Kuriakose Kunnacherry of Kottayam, India. His Address to the Synod in 1987 is included in this volume. Before the Synod, Bishop Kunnacherry prepared a study text, *Deaconess in the Church: A Pastoral Need of the Day?* In it he asks:

> Would the ordination of women to the diaconate positively assist the Church in responding to the demands of the Gospel and the challenge of the contemporary world?
>
> 1. The role of women in our society is changing rapidly in the direction of facing equality with men.
>
> 2. The ministry of women in the Church would be a *new* kind of ministry. This will have patterns and forms of ministry proper to itself. Women would bring a different quality to certain ministries of the Church.
>
> 3. This will be a great boost to the status and dignity of women, especially in the developing countries where religious traditions and cultural values are discriminating against the women.

2

The View from Inside

Virginia Kaib Ratigan

Of the over 9,000 permanent deacons in the United States, 94% are married. To speak of deacons' wives is to speak of women with a variety of perspectives and experiences within the Church. These women, more than any others, would seem from their experience and participation in the diaconate formation programs to have special insight into the diaconate. We began our study by formulating a survey which was sent in late spring, 1988, to five hundred women across the country. We were well aware that there would be diversity of age, background and experience, but just how diverse and personal the individual perceptions of these women would be was not revealed until we read the many comments which accompanied the standardized portion of the questionnaire. We found these to be one of the richest sources for our study.

Even the term "deacon's wife" is problematic to many since it indicates the same mask that feminists have seen in any such title (doctor's wife, professor's wife, etc.). Because our systematic sample was taken from a selected list of names of permanent deacons in the United States, we had no way of determining the names of the women we were trying to contact. Only about 1% of the list we used included the names of both husband and wife, and this, we discovered, was done by only a few dioceses and not necessarily requested by deacons' wives. When asked about this issue, one woman whose name appeared with her husband's on our list replied: "I have no idea why the address for my husband and me is different from anyone else's. . . . In fact, I am very surprised that it is. Our diocese has al-

17

ways been *very* supportive of the *deacon couple* concept. All the mail from the diocese is addressed to the two of us (if it pertains to the deacon program). Wives are invited to virtually every activity . . . .Wives sit on the deacons' board, etc., etc."

At the time we were searching, we could find no readily-available public listing of the wives of permanent deacons in the U.S. Although our survey was directed to them, it was necessary in most cases to send it in care of their husbands. Our roundabout method was a particularly bitter pill to swallow for some of those women whose names did not appear with their husbands' on the mailing list. One respondent says: "Are women as wives of deacons non-existent with no names?" and another, "If this questionnaire is for the wife of a deacon to fill out, why was it addressed to HIM? Many husbands *do not* pass this information on to their wives." One can read the frustration in this woman's reply: "Is it the same case as usual, Deacon Smith and 'what's her name?' " Given the constraints of time and readily-available mailing lists we were both compelled on the one hand and reluctant on the other to approach the questionnaire in this way.

Despite the practical difficulties inherent in a survey approach, there was a great deal of support for our project from many of the respondents. Some went out of their way to wish us good luck on the project and one added, "May the Spirit blow a wind of fresh air into our church." Many thanked us for undertaking the project and a particularly enthusiastic person continued, "It gives me hope that not only will women be ordained to the diaconate in the near future, but also the priesthood."

In order to insure responses from various parts of the country, we used a list which included names from every geographical area. We were advised to do a systematic sample, sending the questionnaire to 500 of the names on our list. In all, 243 responses were returned, a response rate of 51.7%, assuming as stated above, that 94% of all deacons are married.

Some of the background data that was received may help give a general profile of the respondents. Their median age was 52.0, and the median number of years that their husbands had been ordained deacons was 7.0. As for the question of how many children were currently living at home, the median response was 1.0. Out of 243 responses, 33.2% of the women work full-time outside the home, 27.9% work part-time and 37.3% do not work outside the home. The non-codable response was 1.6% (which simply means that some respondents "wrote in" statements other than the yes/no option provided or did not check either response). Our sample showed 22.5% said that they do what would be considered volunteer work, 76.3% do not and the non-codable response was 1.3%.

The results showing the median age of the respondents and average number of children living at home correlates well with the 1988 Report on the Permanent Diaconate in the United States (issued by the National Bishops' Committee on the Permanent Diaconate, Wash., D.C.). That report indicates that 57% of the deacons are between the ages of 51 and 70. Only 35% of the permanent deacons are under 50.

We found that in the area of religion 40.4% of the respondents had had college courses or the equivalent; 9.1% had a college major or minor in religion and 9.1% had had other professional theological studies. Other responses were scattered among parochial grade and high school backgrounds, C.C.D. classes and convert classes. It was interesting to note the number of women who did have advanced study in either religion or a field relating to ministry. In fact, one respondent said: "My husband comments that I should be ordained: (My part-time position is Pastoral Asst.) Also, I am a professional counselor. I have been involved in church-related activities much longer than he. . . and 'minister' in ongoing ways. However, I do not feel called nor desire the diaconate nor priesthood. I support and affirm any women who might." In one informal interview with a deacon's wife, we discovered that she had completed an undergraduate degree in Religious Studies and had already begun classes for an M.A. in Religious Studies. She also mentioned that she had been involved in parish work long before her husband became interested in the permanent diaconate.

In 1979, a *National Study of the Permanent Diaconate in the United States* was authorized by the Bishops' Committee on the Permanent Diaconate (Wash., D.C.) and was sent to every permanent deacon (at that time there were 135 diocesan centers and around 5,000 ordained deacons). There were four phases to the study and Phase Two was directed to the wives of ordained deacons. This questionnaire was designed to determine their attitudes before and after their husbands' ordination. In the ten years since that study, there are some differences in these attitudes which will be noticed as our research unfolds. In the 1979 study, a total of 1282 questionnaires was distributed (the number responded to by deacons in the Phase I segment of the study). There were 696 returned, a 54.3% response rate. Throughout that study specific reference is made to the U.S. Bishops' initial guidelines published in 1971 (*Permanent Deacons in the U.S.: Guidelines on Their Formation and Ministry*). Those sections pertaining to wives are particularly relevant to our study as well:

• A wife must formally consent to her husband's ordination. (119, 150)

• A wife is free to choose or determine the extent to which she will be involved in her husband's ministry. (151, 152)

• Developmental programs for wives are necessary. (129)

• Consideration should be given to the family's economic situation. (130,154)

• Commitment to wife and family has clear priority over ministry. (127)

• Two-way communication between the diocesan office and the deacons' wives is crucial. (128)

It seems valuable to be aware of these *Guidelines* since it becomes obvious from questionnaire responses and from the individual stories of deacons' wives that many women have judged the success or failure of their experience in the diaconate on the basis of these directives.

The experience of deacons' wives has confirmed the larger issue of equality and justice for women in the Church, according to one of our respondents: "Individual archdioceses, clergy, lay people, react in different ways to deacons and deacons' wives. While deacons are now being accepted in a more open manner, wives of deacons are still holding the place that women have always held. The mind/body split of Western culture has placed the feminine within Church tradition as dangerous/material/sinful. Changes are slow within the Church, and women, whatever their role in society, as wife, widow, single, divorced parent, mother, sister, daughter or nun, cannot claim full personhood within the Church."

This question of identity and personhood continues to plague many of the women. As one woman put it, "I feel resentful because I feel that the Church acquires two bodies to work for the Church when they ordain a deacon and doesn't actively provide any support or development for the deacon's wife. The Church gets two for the price of one and it does make me very angry. I was extremely active with church work prior to my husband's ordination, and I have gradually backed away from all my involvements. I guess I feel a sense of being used." One of our respondents from the Hispanic community said that she and her deacon husband considered themselves two mature Catholics serving the community which affirmed and supported them. However, she said, "I do not see that same recognition of persons and acceptance of a family's role in the diaconate program within the Archdiocese, especially from the Office of the Diaconate. The idea of a male clergy is so set in the Church that I believe that deacons are treated as married priests and their wives are ignored as though we are invisible. Sometimes I feel like a tag-along to my husband's once-in-awhile social functions with deacons. When the diaconate office does attempt to communicate with me, I find it insulting to be considered 'esposa' rather than as a woman who has a sense of dignity as an adult Catholic." Although the *Guidelines* listed earlier promoted an ideal relationship between the deacons' spouses and diocesan administration, it seems as if the fulfillment is a long way off for some. It seems safe to say from the comments we received that some women do feel degraded in their position.

The guideline that insisted that "consideration should be given to the family's economic situation" was also a source of deep concern for some respondents. One respondent noted that the diaconate is a "volunteer position." "Our personal experience is that between 25-30 hours per week are given to the service of deacon. We have a young family, trying to provide a Catholic education for each . . . . We find this a financial burden. Why is the diaconate the only ordained ministry that does not provide remuneration for service? I have only started working outside our family business since my husband's ordination—this is to provide financial support in addition to moral support." In another comment, the analogy is all too familiar: "I have come to feel that deacons are much like housewives. Because they are not paid, many people do not value the work performed." An older woman reflects on the issue: "I would not have wanted my husband in the diaconate when the children were very young. It takes two paychecks for most young couples to get by. I strongly believe that it would be a strain on her marriage for a working wife with children." Another person insists: "I suggest you also look into how the diaconate has affected the families financially. Deacons and deacon families are very generous with their time, talent, possessions. We went through financial 'hell' by trying to rearrange our life by what we believe the Lord was calling us to do. We know *many* other deacon families who also experience great financial difficulties. . . .It's so sad to see good families bringing the gospel message to others, when they in turn have a very difficult time providing Catholic education for their own children."

We included a series of questions in the survey that would indicate how many women attended diaconate preparation classes. The first question in that series asked whether or not the arch/diocese *required* attendance of the deacon's wife. Out of 211 responding, 22.7% replied "Yes," 74.9% replied "No" and 2.9% of the responses were non-codable. The next question asked if the arch/diocese *recommended* attendance at class. As expected, there were a fairly large number of programs which recommended attendance. Out of 214 responses, 73.4% replied "Yes," 24.3% "No" and 2.3% of the responses were non-codable. The next two questions were designed to discover how many women actually attended classes and to what extent they felt that attending the classes expanded their knowledge. Out of 243 responses, 40.3% said that they "always" attended and the numbers ranged downward to 14.0% who seldom or never attended. A fairly large number felt that their knowledge had been expanded by participation in the program. Of 234 responses, 46.6% said that their knowledge was "greatly" expanded, 32.1% "to a considerable extent" and the numbers ranged down to 0.9% who responded "not at all."

Participation in the diaconal preparation program was the subject of several individual comments on the questionnaire. When one thinks of the amount of time involved, with literally no recognition for the work, it is easy to understand the following comment: "If I had had the opportunity to become a deacon at the same time as my husband, I probably would have attended classes with him and worked at preparing myself." Along the same lines, another woman said: "Encouraged/urged to attend the preparation classes their husbands are required to attend, wives gain no recognition within the structure itself. Wives of deacons are tolerated as necessary parts of the deacon influx into the clergy structure of the church, but women are still feared, mistrusted, misunderstood and relegated to the 'helper' role." Another strain of disillusionment shows itself in this comment: "After three years of study, it was very difficult at ordination not to be included in any pictures. We strongly felt that it was a couple ministry and found that many people began to recognize my husband and that I no longer counted. Eventually I rebuilt my own ministry." One woman said that she took all the courses. "When it came time for the first final exam I asked to take it. The director of the program laughed in my face. I was not the only wife who took all the classes. I *was* the only one who asked that my attendance be recognized by taking the tests. Needless to say, I was never given an exam." Another person suggests that "priests need to start thinking men *and* women" in the deacon education program. One woman reported that "no support system was given to enable the wife to attend classes—I resented my husband leaving for three-day weekends, and I had to care for young children after working all week. Part of the weekend included a four-hour meeting which the wife *was not allowed to attend*." This theme of lack of concern for family and downright exclusion from events was noted in many of the comments.

Not all of the reaction to participation in diaconal courses (when suggested or required) was negative. One woman perceived the experience as a growth opportunity, saying that "it gave us the chance to grow spiritually together." In another situation, the diocese recognized full participation in a "Pastoral Ministry Program" which two wives completed with their husbands. It was clear that the woman responding was actively involved in parish ministry. Another respondent discovered that her participation in the courses updated her understanding of the church and she felt better informed. "I enjoyed the classes I did get to. . . .I felt a camaraderie with the wives." Several others commented on the good quality of the courses and one respondent mentioned that the courses in her diocesan program were taken at the Episcopal Seminary with the deacon candidates there.

Participation in diaconal courses was often a great hardship for many women. Those with small children spoke of how the family had to juggle schedules to meet the classes and weekend sessions required by the program. "I have had multiple sclerosis for 33 years of our 35 years of marriage," wrote one woman. "I fully participated in all diaconal schooling and activities—wheelchair-bound all through formation."

The issue of diaconal work was another important question in our study. We asked: Do you find that because your husband is a deacon you have also done diaconal work?

a) Leading Prayer	n=232	%
Yes	77	33.2%
No	153	65.9%
Non-codable response	2	0.9%
b) Preaching	n=204	%
Yes	26	12.7%
No	173	84.8%
Non-codable response	5	2.5%
c) Ministry to the Sick	n=229	%
Yes	95	40.9%
No	130	56.0%
Non-codable response	4	1.7%
d) Counseling	n=221	%
Yes	115	49.6%
No	102	44.0%
Non-codable response	4	1.7%

The results of this section of the study are not surprising, given the high percentage of women who did participate in the deacon formation program with their husbands and/or have done further studies in theology and ministry independently. The numbers also suggest both the struggle in many smaller communities to find anyone at all to do the work and the fact that many women claim to have been doing what would be considered diaconal work before their husbands' ordination.

The questionnaire shows that 33.2% of the respondents are leading prayer services. The comments show that these services are varied in content and context. For example, one might lead a morning communion service in the parish when the pastor and deacon are away while another works in the context of a nursing home. Some respondents said that prayer services were a part of the C.C.D. program in which they were teaching. "My husband and I have been leading prayer services in our home long before he was ordained a deacon," another commented.

Among the 12.7% of the respondents who said that they were doing preaching, there was no clear indication of when or where this was being done. We learned that some women felt prepared to preach as a result of their own theological/pastoral education and felt that they would do a much better job, given the opportunity. The strain on women that comes with suppressing this gift came through in several of these remarks.

Judging from both informal conversation with deacons' wives and questionnaire comments, the work of visiting the sick and counseling is an integral part of everyday life. Some women are already eucharistic ministers in their parishes and take communion to the sick on a regular basis. Others say that they have become involved in situations where there is critical illness or devastating accidents. Their "presence" has been perceived as diaconal to the extent that some families have assumed that the one standing by them was herself a "deacon." "The families have become our friends," says one person. "These are the people who strongly support deacons—some ask if I am a nun or deacon." Regular visits to hospitals and nursing homes had been part of the weekly schedule for some women before their husbands' ordination. Others joined in the work after ordination.

The largest number of women responding positively to doing what might be considered diaconal work was in the area of counseling (49.6%). The range of this activity was wide: some have earned professional degrees in counseling and are active on parish pastoral ministry teams; others counsel in geriatric centers, hospitals and in school settings; one has her own practice; others find lending a compassionate ear has become a way of life. Another woman speaks of a ministry that she sees as informal counseling. "We have taken children (5) at one time while Mom was in the hospital, a young woman with two children, elderly man and teenager for various lengths of time in our home as a result of my husband's ministry."

In addition to diaconal work, a number of the respondents indicated that they were actively involved in supportive work primarily in the communicating and relaying of messages and helping to facilitate meetings and social gatherings. "Wives, I am learning, run the gamut from non-interest in their husbands' ministry to suffocating involvement," writes one respondent. "I would like to see some wives free to pursue their own specialness and the Church accept wives and the roles they play in facilitating their husbands' ministries."

When asked how they felt about doing the work related to their husbands' diaconate, 83% were happy in general with the situation; 8% felt like a "deacon" without a title; 3% were resentful of the situation; 8% were uncertain; and there was a 2% non-codable response.

We also learned that out of 242 responses, 82.6% of the women were active before their husbands' involvement. This fact is not surprising, given U.S. diocesan structures with their dependence on volunteer work (including teaching, parish ministries, and hospital work). In both the past and the present, this volunteer work has been done primarily by women. In individual comments, some women expressly stated that their own church work was independent of the support services which they gave to their husbands. One respondent who seemed quite content with the relationship between her own work and her husband's diaconate clearly stated that she would seek ordination. "I was called to be a chaplain in a maternity hospital for the poor. I believe if I were ordained I would have a more professional status and acceptance by staff and employees, although I have had no problems and the patients accept me. Perhaps it's my own goal to be more or be able to serve more."

Some respondents even commented that they were a bit resentful that "he" came on the work later and was officially recognized for work that they had already been doing. One of the respondents said that "many wives were the 'deacon' in our class. They did the work while their husbands were the ones ordained and recognized by the Church. The women did the service work—much more compassionately and spirit-filled than their spouses."

Although much can be learned about the activities of deacons' wives today, our questionnaire was not focused primarily in that direction. Our intentions were to gain insight and perspective on the actual functioning (successes and failures) of the diaconate from those individuals who have a special first-hand awareness of the work involved. The issue of whether or not these respondents supported the ordination of women to the diaconate became an important question, given their practical experience both independently and in the context of their husbands' diaconal work. We felt it quite important to separate the question of whether or not deacons' wives were in favor of a diaconate for women from the question of whether they might personally feel called to the diaconate if present legislation of the Church were to change. The *National Study* asked only the latter question. (In 1979, out of 144 responses, there was indication that seven would personally want to be deacon(esses)—5% of the total.) We have no way of knowing how many would have supported the diaconate for women.

As a matter of fact, we began to see this important distinction through the eyes of a deacon's wife who recalled that in speaking with several women in a current session of diaconal formation, they were beginning to put two and two together and ask the question "Why not ordain women?" It was less a case of feeling that they might want this personally than their perception, through their own participation in the program, that women were perfectly competent to do the work.

There are two items on our survey instrument that relate to these.

1. How do you feel about women in the permanent diaconate?

	n=243	%
Do not approve	65	26.7%
Approve, but do not feel called	142	58.4%
Approve, would be a deacon, lack time .	6	2.5%
Would like to be a deacon in the future .	10	4.1%

Interested in diaconal ordination now . .	9	3.7%
Non-codable response	11	4.5%

2. If you approve of women deacons, when did you come to that conclusion?

	n=180	%
Before your husband began training . .	54	30.0%
While your husband was in training . .	49	27.2%
Since your husband's ordination	67	37.2%
Non-codable response	10	5.6%

Of the 26.7% who did not approve of the permanent diaconate for women, several voiced clear and strong opinions. One woman called the whole idea "heresy," while another said, "I am strongly against women in the diaconate and/or priesthood. Mary, our Blessed Mother, has the highest place in Heaven next to her Son. On earth she was *obedient* to *God's will*." The realism of her own situation prompted a third to conclude, "The diaconate has a long way to come in our area—many priests have a hard time dealing with other men—deacons—much less women. . . and don't even know what to do with deacons' wives, much less women deacons." Another stated that "the ordination of a woman deacon would be a great conflict in the Catholic Church." Yet another said: "Our church has not instituted ordination of women to permanent diaconate and I agree with the wisdom of our church." A slightly different tack was taken in this comment: "I am not in favor of ordained women, deacons or priests. Insecure women need a title." Finally a more basic concern was expressed when one person said, "I believe that the Church has not yet established a theology of the diaconate as far as male deacons are concerned and I feel this should be accomplished before women are ordained." This was a woman whose husband had been in the diaconate for eight years and who had herself been doing volunteer work in her diocese for over fourteen years.

The issue of "time" was the focus of a few comments. "The role of 'deacon' is very time-consuming" wrote one respondent. "I do not feel that a woman who is wife, mother, homemaker, and works outside the home could ever do justice to the job of deacon. But some of the nuns and women who are not married could carry out the role of deacon. Although I do not believe we are ready for women leaders in our church."

Some of the opposition that some deacons' wives have to the idea of a diaconate for women is based on the very real difficulties they have experienced at the parish level. They have been pained by the lack of recognition and acceptance of their deacon husbands by both clergy and laity.

From the other side of the issue, it has been shown in the survey that out of 243 responses, 68.7% approve of women deacons in one way or another. This may reflect the growing acceptance in general of the ordination of women to the permanent diaconate. For example, in May 1986, *U.S. Catholic* conducted a poll from a representative sample of their subscribers. At that time, 62% agreed that the diaconate should be open to women as well as men. This we know is not a simple matter since significant opposition to the diaconate has been voiced by feminists, as discussed in Section 1.

In our survey, support for the ordination of women to the permanent diaconate was significantly strong. Said one respondent: "I am certainly in favor of ordination of women to the permanent diaconate (those who feel called). The Church would be richer by taking this step." Another who was personally in favor of women in the diaconate describes her Northwest diocese as a "large island mass with small numbers of people. The difficulty in this diocese is that there is not any travel possible except by plane or boat." She noted that their diocese is dependent primarily on missionary priests and that the diaconate has been temporarily discontinued because of problems of integrating deacons into the present structure. Despite these problems, "Our Bishop does say that he would ordain women to the diaconate." From another perspective, a respondent wanted to "reaffirm a role for women in ministry—they are more sensitive to people's needs. The right person would make a good deacon." One woman explained she had come to favor women's ordination to the diaconate since her husband's ordination. "I saw a definite need in parish life for ordained women ministers attached to a particular community and called to serve God's people in very unique ways."

Is the struggle worthwhile? One woman wrote: "Because all the baptized can do most of the things deacons do, it is possible to live a diaconal life, but it doesn't quite satisfy: many of us who feel called to this ministry carry some anger about our exclusion. I believe that women bring another dimension to ministry and another outlook to preaching. We image our God in other ways that can be helpful to people. Sometimes I feel that I don't want to buy into the system which I feel is seriously flawed, but another part of me says that the reformers need to get as many noses in the tent as possible to effect change." Another reply was based on the stark reality of "need." "I worry about small parishes like ours in the future; we have only 250 people and an older priest who is quite ill. Will these parishes be closed rather than rely on deacons and women? It would be a shame if that happened."

It is interesting to note that seven women from the earlier survey would seek ordination to the permanent diaconate if it were offered. Perhaps the ten intervening years gave women a clearer sense of what is involved in diaconal work. Or it might be that many women recognized the work that they were already doing as diaconal work. Another aspect to consider is the fact that our survey indicates a median age slightly older than the earlier survey and also determines that the median number of children at home is 1.0. This is a very significant factor when considering this issue. Younger women who perceived themselves as doing diaconal work alongside their husbands tended to feel guilty about leaving their younger children, whereas older women found that their circumstances were right for such involvement. In addition, those ten years generally reveal a greater consciousness among women of their own gifts and potential, despite the slow pace of change in both Church and society. By the time our survey reached deacons'wives in 1989, six women wanted to be deacons but felt they lacked time, ten wanted to be deacons in the future and nine were interested in diaconal ordination now.

One woman shared an intimate reflection on her situation. In it one sees how the situation erodes the human spirit. "I went through an identity crisis six months prior to ordination and dealt with it. . . . At one time I badly wanted to be a deacon. Now I'm not so sure. . . . I suspect that even if ordained, women would not be treated equally and it is not easy being a 'pioneer.' However, I strongly endorse the idea of women deacons and consider it a justice issue. As I look back, I honestly wonder if I really wanted to be a deacon or if I just wanted the opportunity to say, 'no, thank you.' The Diaconate Director told me at one time that if women were ever ordained I would be first in line in our diocese. Now I am not sure how I would respond. Without ordination, without title and without authorization, I feel like a deacon and I know I do diaconal work."

The idea of being a "pioneer" was taken up by another respondent. "After children and their educational demands are off the family budget, there might be enough time and energy to pursue a *pioneering* ministry. I have had contacts with female Anglican priests and Methodist ministers and a Catholic Ph.D. that were all functioning on the same level in different churches. However, all were single women with grown or no children in their homes and all had to become very aggressive to hold their ministerial positions as women in a pioneering call within this century of Church. I see a great need for women's work in the Church and am looking forward to the day of ordination of women deacons."

The question of how well deacons are received in their parishes also plays a part in what the women in our study are thinking and feeling about the permanent diaconate for women. The results show that very few women have confidence that women would be accepted in the parish as deacons by either laity or clergy. The comments show that the problems that women have encountered with their husbands in parish work and at diocesan administration levels have left a bad taste in the mouth and so the risk may simply not be worth it.

Our study would not be complete without a look at the relation of the deacon couple to one another and their relationship to the larger community. Apparently there is a great deal of diversity in perception and experience with regard to this issue. In general, our survey indicates that 86% of the women feel secure in their present situation. The comments go much further in uncovering the meaning of that statement.

There is one line of development which seeks to emphasize the individuality of the couple. "I feel that the call to be a deacon for a man or woman is a separate and individual call and not necessarily related to marriage. I'm happy for the gifts and growth he has experienced, but feel free to develop my own gifts and service myself. My husband does not expect me to be his shadow. We have enjoyed the spiritual and educational opportunities available in the program together and separately." The same theme is present in a response which comments on the question of the women doing diaconal work. "I feel that my participation in those activities is not because my husband is a deacon. My personal spiritual growth and development are not predicated on my husband's diaconal vocation. While we have been married for 37 years and are devoted to each other, we each feel responsibility for continuing spiritual growth and do not think that such an important part of our lives should solely be the responsibility of one partner." Another woman writes concerning the various ministries she performs, "I do these various ministries not because my husband is a deacon but because of who I am. I did them before he was ordained and will continue no matter what he chooses to do." There is a clear sense of the potential difficulties that diaconate can bring to a relationship in this statement: "I don't feel I had a calling to ministry when my husband was called to the Diaconate—as some wives feel. My husband is the ordained deacon and I think of my role as only in a supportive capacity (which involves quite a bit).

There are those who feel quite differently and envision a future in the church for a collaborative ministry—a reality which is in effect now but has yet to be officially recognized. "My husband and I see ourselves called to ministry as a team and believe this flows from our sacrament of Matrimony. With the exception of some liturgical ministries, we operate as a team. We are listed on the front of our bulletin as Diaconate Team." In this case our respondent felt that if she "were to take on any public and permanent commitment, it would place a strain on us and would involve much discernment, as did our original discussion and discernment, about diaconate." Along those same lines, it is the experience of another couple that "our pastor sort of looks at the diaconate as being a dual-ministry (with exception of assisting at Mass). We work as a couple in baptism preparation and currently for the next three years (as couple) will be assisting in a general census of the parish. We both attend a monthly staff meeting—we are both involved in the RCIA program."

The idea of a deacon couple—both ordained—is one which appears to be credible to a number of women who have written comments. "My husband and I see no reason why husband and wife could not both enjoy the special charism of the diaconate and use it to witness to the spreading of the kingdom," writes a woman who sees many needs being unmet in her present situation. The realization of these unmet needs is the bottom line for many who chose to tell us more about their situation.

In the spectrum of these questionnaires, there is still a sense of the older pre-Vatican II Church, as well as the Church in the modern world. The tensions on issues of authority, liturgy, education and pastoral ministry are all present. The honesty with which respondents revealed their experiences—their thoughts, hopes and dreams—is a treasured source of information for us. As the question of a diaconate for women is evaluated at this juncture of the Church's life, let the voices of these women be a respected source of wisdom for future decisions.

3

On the High Desert of the Southwest

Catherine Stewart-Roache

To understand my story of the diaconate, it is necessary to know a bit about New Mexico in the early 1970s. At that time the entire state was one archdiocese: very large, very diversified in ages, ethnic backgrounds, economic and social conditions. The archbishop, James Peter Davis, was a man of contrasts and complexities. A man excited by Vatican II, with bold pastoral ideas as well as intense loyalties to clergy. In 1972 the reviving of the diaconate in the form of ordination of permanent deacons was an occasion for him to respond to the needs of his vast and complex archdiocese and the dream of a young priest, Spencer Stopa, who became the first director of the deacon training program of the Archdiocese of Santa Fe.

Spence Stopa was a friend of mine. We used to talk (or was it "dialogue" in those days?) about Vatican II, scripture, celibacy, married priests, and women in the Church. In these discussions it became clear that he saw the situation of women within the Church as being unequal and unjust—a reality which was becoming painfully clear to me. When he prepared to send out the call for applicants to the second class of permanent deacons, I challenged him: "You have convinced me that you see a need for women to be ordained as priests or deacons—need for the Church as well as for women—are you personally willing to move this along? Are you willing to include women in the deacon training program?"

34

After some thought (and I'd guess prayer because he took praying seriously), he said that he could and that he would. He didn't do much consulting with "superiors," he simply sent out the notice that applications of men and women wishing to become permanent deacons were being considered by the Deacon Board.

To his surprise, and mine, 16 women applied. I was one of them. This decision was difficult and easy. Difficult because it would mean moving into a big unknown, spending time away from my five children and husband, and becoming very public as a feminist. This was a new and rather uncomfortable identity for me at the time. After all, I was a happy wife and mother of five; did I want to put myself and my family through what I couldn't predict or control?

The easy part was that being ordained—if that time ever came—would feel so natural. I knew that it would not come at the end of the training program, but someday it would. When that time came it would be the culmination of what I had known to be my calling since I was a girl. I had no vocation to become a Sister, but I had always wanted to be ordained. This seemed to be a step in responding to that call. My husband listened to my arguments with myself and supported me in my decision to apply.

During the spring, while all this was happening to me and 15 other women in the archdiocese, a new bishop was appointed, Robert F. Sanchez (he would be installed on July 25, 1975). During the early part of the summer, he was asked by the permanent deacons and Spence Stopa if he planned to do anything about the women who had applied for the next class of deacons. At that time he said "no"; he was aware that there was no other means for women to be trained for ministry, and he was supportive of women being more involved in ministry in the archdiocese; he saw himself as enthusiastic about Vatican II concepts of participation of the People of God in the work of the Church.

Those were his summer thoughts. The process of testing and selection moved along. Psychological tests were given the applicants, and the women came through as very sound candidates. By December there were still five of us who were ready to begin the program, which was to start the first week of January. Then, without discussion or warning, the bishop said that he had "changed his mind." No women were to be included in the deacon training program.

I was shocked that such a unilateral decision could be made without consultation with the director, the deacon board, or the women involved. My only recourse was to do what I did best—take a LONG walk in the mountains and pray and shout to God. Like Isaiah in times past, I discovered that "On the mountain, God provides." As a result, I decided to contact the deacon board, a body which existed to advise the archbishop on matters pertaining to the deacon program and permanent deacons in our area. It seemed to me that I had a right to bring our case before them, and give them the opportunity to tell the archbishop that he had made a mistake and advise him of the need for women to be in the program because we were qualified applicants, because it would be a just thing to do, and because the archdiocese needed our ministry.

The board agreed to meet with me. I went to the priest who was sponsoring me for the diaconate, and he tried to talk me out of going. He thought it would be a useless gesture. I asked him if he was coming with me or not. He said he would come, but not to get my hope up.

It was a very difficult three-hour meeting. Some were opposed to our being in the class because they "did not want to be responsible for our mental health" when the end came and we were not ordained with the men. Others said it wasn't the right time; still others thought it would be too difficult for "some" priests to accept. As the clock ticked on, it looked less and less likely that this would be a moment of a small breakthrough in the sexist structures of *ecclesia*. Then a young priest, who had been silent most of the evening, said, "I am ashamed that women must beg in our church." He spoke only a short time; he touched the hearts of the board members in ways that my logic had failed to do.

The vote to accept us as applicants passed unanimously. The board advised the archbishop and he decided to say nothing. The new director of the program responded to us as to any other members of the class when we assembled in January. We signed the same letter of intent to be ordained as did the men in the class.

In the beginning of what was to become the class of 1978, there were about 28, five women and 23 men. By the end of the almost four years, the men's numbers dropped to about half, but the women remained constant. We were Linda Chavez, the head of the theology department at our only Catholic high school in Albuquerque and a member of the Sisters of Charity (Cincinnati); Mary Cates, a member of the Third Order of Carmel, Discalced, whose ministry was with frail elderly people in Santa Fe; Joan Cain, also a Sister of Charity and a minister to the sick; Liz Cullen and Paula Houlihan, wives of permanent deacon candidates who wanted the training in ministry offered by the program. At the time, I was a minister of the Eucharist who was coordinating other eucharistic ministers in their response to the needs of elderly people in nursing and boarding homes.

1975 was an important year for women all over the world. During this International Year of the Woman, women began to think new thoughts, and to think old thoughts in new ways. Spring of 1975 saw the emergence of the first Women's Ordination Conference, held in Detroit. Linda Chavez and I went to this conference because we saw the ordination of women to the Permanent Diaconate as part of the ordination issue. We were feeling hopeful and good at that time. Our classmates were supportive, our teachers were, too, and the new archbishop had sent a telegram to the conference wishing us well and offering his prayers for our deliberations.

This spirit held through the fall of 1975, and at the time of the ceremony for what used to be called "minor orders," when the men were ordained to be Ordinary Ministers of the Eucharist and Readers, the five of us read a statement of our readiness and willingness to minister in these ways. By this time it was clear that we were women who had a lot of experience in ministry and generally had had much more theology than most of the men in the class. But it was equally clear that we were the wrong sex. That was the only impediment. As the archbishop refused to ordain us he prayed that "someday the work of the Holy Spirit would reach completion."

During the following months and years this spirit was seriously eroded. Many factors contributed to this. The director of the program changed several times; each was less understanding and supportive of the women participants. Finally, there was outright hostility. I myself had to deal with four changes in sponsors. My last sponsor worked in Las Vegas, New Mexico, and I had to drive 200 miles there and back every week to fulfill the internship requirement.

At the same time, the archbishop was feeling more and more uncomfortable with his bold actions of 1975; the Pope's letter concerning ordination of women had been issued and Sanchez did not want to appear as contradicting anything contained in that document.

Personally, we women in the training program were doing all right. The course work had not been difficult, we had support and love from our families and communities and from those with whom we ministered. I was enjoying the stimulation of continuing my education by pursuing a Doctor of Ministry degree. (I was also completing the course work necessary for my equivalent Master in Divinity degree required as a prerequisite for the doctorate.)

As part of this degree, I worked with another doctoral candidate on the liturgy for the permanent deacon ordination ceremony which was to be held on May 20, 1978 at the cathedral in Santa Fe. He was a priest, apparently sympathetic to our situation, and Liturgist for the archbishop. We worked well together and came up with a ceremony which would recognize the ministry of women by our being commissioned as Ministers of Christian Service; we would also be visible as part of the class and as candidates for ordination whenever that might occur in the future.

That was the plan. The reality was very different. Again, without any communication or warning, changes were made. We showed up at the cathedral with our classmates who were being lined up in alphabetical order. We were told to "go to the end of the processional line" because "we don't want it to look like you are part of the class, or being ordained." The men were given candles to hold which would be extinguished when they were ordained and themselves became lights of God's word to the people. We were given none, but we *were* given the irony and joy of the Gospel for the day which urged us not to put our light under a bushel basket, but to shine—anyway.

The ceremony was long and painful to me, especially when it came time for the homily. Robert Sanchez said that he was addressing the men, not the women; he would address us later, during the commissioning ceremony.

Just a note about this commissioning ceremony. It was one developed by Bishop Charles Buswell of Pueblo, Colorado, which he used instead of the ordination to the diaconate ritual, because women would be excluded from an ordination, but not a commissioning ceremony. Women in this country have no better friend than Charlie Buswell. He not only intellectually is committed to equality and justice for women, he has the love and courage to act in creative ways.

After Holy Communion, our ceremony began. The archbishop called us up, one by one, to be blessed and receive a Bible as a symbol of our service to the people of the archdiocese and our commitment to the Word of God. Even this was a painful moment because someone had forgotten to buy us Bibles and they used the same paperback for all of us. (We were told that individual Bibles would be given to us later; to this day, none of us has received them.)

Each of us was called forward; since my name began with an "S," I was to be last. My heart beat furiously as I saw four women go up, kneel before the bishop, kiss his ring, and silently return to our places. Throughout the mass I had been troubled by the brokenness of the day, troubled by the mixed messages about women in the Church being given to all assembled. A voice within me was telling me that I must speak out and that this was the time and the place for the folks to hear a woman speak IN church.

When my name was called, I walked up to Robert Sanchez and stood in front of him as I had many times when we simply talked together. This was not a time to kneel before him or kiss his ring. He gave me the traditional *abrazo* and asked about my husband and children. I looked at him and said, "Robert, I have something to say and I need your microphone." He was very surprised and paused; he said, "Do you have to?" I replied, "Yes."

My statement was brief. I turned to the people and said that I had come from a state where the legislators had tried to convince us that equality could be achieved with a policy of "separate but equal." I said that I had come to know that that is not possible in a state or in a church and that I prayed for the day that the Holy Spirit of God could blow freely among women and men and true equality would be a reality for all. As I finished, I was shaking but felt a tremendous sense of peace.

The cathedral burst into applause. Now I was the one who was surprised. It went on for a long time. Finally, the archbishop started laughing and said, "I guess the people have spoken." He knew that they were registering their approval of our being commissioned as ministers in any form.

We left the altar. So many stopped to talk and shake our hands that the procession was disrupted and the archbishop had to pass us and leave ahead of us—protocol was broken. Old women and young, Hispanic and others, spoke to us and one old woman said, "I never thought I would live to see the day anyone spoke about justice WITHIN the church."

Like Mary, I have kept these words in my heart, treasured them and pondered them. They have sustained me through ten years. Years which have called for assertiveness in ministry because not one of us was ever contacted by the chancery or our parishes to act as "Ministers of Christian Service." But we have ministered just the same. We have continued what we were doing before 1974-78 and some have moved into new areas. For five years, I was the chaplain at a local nondenominational hospital. This was very satisfying work but it brought out to me more clearly that my vocation is to priestly sacramental ministry. It made no sense for me to minister with people during sometimes painful moments and then have to call in a stranger to administer the sacraments of the sick, or reconciliation. It seemed then, and now, to be far from the insights of Vatican II. When I was a young girl I heard strong comments about men and women who "lived together" without the benefit of the sacrament of matrimony. The grace of this sacrament which I have been living for 25 years now was, and still is, of importance to those who study theology, scriptures and doctrine. It seems obvious to me that what the official Church is doing is asking women to do is to live in sin—to live without the "benefit of the sacrament," in this case the sacrament of Holy Orders. It is a sinful situation because it is a broken sign of the whole body of Christ, it is a broken sign of the words of baptism when boy and girl babies, men and women are charged as "priest, prophet, king." I believe that this is the prophetic time to take these words seriously. Women, and all of the Church, need the sign of ordained women (permanent deacons and priests) and leaders of all sorts—not kings or queens, but ones who can be catalysts for the spirit of God, like the salt of the earth mentioned in scripture.

Ordaining women is not the solution, but it is a necessary part of the process of healing the brokenness produced by sexism which is preventing a recognition of the vocation of so many women who know they have been called by God for sacramental ministry. All other Christian denominations have had to struggle with the issue of women in official, graced positions. I know many ordained Christian ministers; their struggles for understanding, support, and justice did not end when they were ordained. But the people of their congregations and denominations have a sign that as women and men limited by a sexist history, struggling for truth and wholeness, we women are included in the process and share the responsibility and power to change structures which need changing if God's Word is to live in this time, this place, these hearts and minds.

Some days I think of Joan of Arc. She had a call from God to a powerful, misunderstood ministry. If we read through transcripts of her trial we find alarm that she was acting and dressing like a man; to the ecclesiastical authorities and some theologians, leadership was not proper for a woman, no matter how gifted and graced. The Church itself was the one who condemned her and prevented her from fully responding to her vocation. Are we going to watch the Church repeat mistakes of the past? Or is now the time for the Church to pause and consider that perhaps the Spirit of God is moving in new ways in our lives, that God is indeed still capable of bringing forth something new in the desert? And those of us who await the fullness of God's actions are encouraged by ancient words: "They that hope in God will renew their strength; they will soar as with eagles' wings; they will run and not be weary, walk and not grow faint."

42 A New Phoebe

To live in the high desert of the Southwest is a particular grace for making those words sound familiar and alive. Eagles abound. We run and walk. I cycle and pray. And wait. We wait. The Church waits.

4

Standing with My People

Joanne Sullivan, S.H.C.J.

How often have I been asked: "Do you want to be a priest?" This is an old question and one I will no longer allow to distract my attention from a vision of the church that reaches beyond "office" or "office-holder." Today I listen to and discern the call to ordained ministry from the people of God and from the depths of my own heart. Where has "listening" brought me? Where does the truth lead me?

I remember quite distinctly my response to the question of ordination when confronted with it in the past. An unequivocal "NO" was my answer. That "no" reflected a constricted perspective of priesthood, a priesthood rooted in parochialism, tied down with administration and bound to an authoritarian hierarchy. I realized that I was not at that time called to parish priesthood. This decision was both comfortable and right for the time.

I have been a member of the Society of the Holy Child Jesus for 35 years. During these years, the Society has moved from the secure structures of the 1950s to the restlessness of the 60s, into the revolution and renewal of the 70s. This community of women enters the 1990s as a congregation with vision, one that holds a world-view that is Incarnational and possesses a freedom that comes from risk-taking, self-determination and a life due to its charism.

"God has chosen to need men and women in every age to reveal his love, to make known the reality of the Incarnation." This opening sentence in our Constitutions impels me to listen once again to the people of God, to my own heart, to God's call within the church.

It has been within the context and life-style of a Sister of the Holy Child that I have been gifted with a worldview that emphasizes inclusion rather than exclusion, connectedness rather than separateness, mutuality, not submission and dominance.

So the question returns: "Do you want to be a priest?" Moving from the formal classroom to parish ministry as a Director of Religious Education and now to Campus Ministry at a Catholic women's college, the call to participate more fully in the sacramental life of the church burns deeply within my life. Life experience becomes the catalyst that fans the flame.

Allow me to speak of two recent incidents that give credence to a call to ordained ministry. At Rosemont College we have two Sunday evening Eucharistic liturgies. On one Sunday the priest was unable to come. The reaction of the waiting student congregation was spontaneous. "Sister, you can lead the liturgy." There was a direct call to me from the community gathered. I remember feeling a deep sense of gratitude to the community, to God. God speaks through the people.

There was another occasion when I was explaining the difficulty I was experiencing in finding priests for daily Eucharist. One person very simply recalled times when either myself or another woman presided at liturgy and said, "You can preside." The reaction from the group gathered was positive, more than positive: "You know us," "You are close to us," "We appreciate having a woman lead us in prayer."

As a human person, I am sensitive to the needs of other persons. In my personal searching, pondering, reflecting, the cry of the poor is the cry of women who have been told that they cannot follow the call to an ordained ministry. It is in sensing the needs of the community in which I live and minister, and then knowing I cannot reach out either sacramentally or structurally, that the pain and frustration of many women becomes my pain. Yet, I find strength and hope in knowing I am not alone. I am convinced that the church, which is God's doing, will be energized with new vitality for life. Death and dying always precede resurrection.

I respond to a new sense of call and mission within the church. The New Testament image of church is that all are brothers and sisters within the community. Some among us have special tasks, definite charisms, and offices. Our brothers and sisters in the Christian community call us to these offices. I believe we are at a turning point, women and men knowing connectedness and mutuality, called together in our church to special ministries. I want to share the sacramental life by being a minister of the sacrament. I long to proclaim the gospel and preach that Word at a Eucharistic liturgy. Living the charism of the Sisters of the Holy Child gives me both the right and the privilege to "Make known the reality of the Incarnation . . . helping others to believe God lives and acts in them and in our world, to rejoice in God's presence."

Ordination—called to orders! There has been a new revelation to me that this can be possible. The diaconate can be a viable ministry for women and men in the church community. Within the diaconate I can proclaim the Word. I feel the urgency to be a sacramental presence to people, to know a call that has come from community, to be the church's official presence among these people. As a woman minister in a women's college, I can hear needs of women, speak with them and for them. I do not presume to be exclusive or sexist, for I am rooted firmly in the belief that men and women must and should work side by side. Imagine the wealth of experience that we would bring to our ministries as we complement one another.

So I return to my original question. Do I want to be ordained? Yes, I do. From the first time that question was posed to me at least ten years ago until this moment I have literally traveled many miles. From Philadelphia to Oregon. From the church in Southern California to West Africa to experiencing church in the Midwest and now coming full circle to Philadelphia.

I have rejoiced with those who rejoice and I have suffered with those in pain. I continue to love the church, yet have been pained by that church. But I live in hope and that hope comes from the community here at Rosemont College and the Society of the Holy Child Jesus. My college gives me the strength to pursue the stirrings of a heart called to orders in the church. The religious community gives me the freedom to find that place where God needs women to make known God's presence.

As a woman of the church of 1990 and beyond, I know I cannot be passive, submissive, or separate. I cannot remain stationary, but must move beyond the security of permanency and predictability into the world that Jesus calls a world of justice and freedom, a world of peace and love. I look forward to a day when women as well as men will be able to respond to the call of God and God's people. I, too, want to know that I can stand with my people, know I have been chosen from among them, ordained by the church for service.

5

Called to Service in the Afro-American Community

Mary C. Shelly

The fundamental ministry of a deacon is a ministry of service. As the wife of a deacon, I share in this ministry because I am the extension and supportive arm of his ministry. On November 30, 1985, I signed a *Letter of Consent* document, requested by the Archdiocese of New Orleans, granting my consent and affirmation to my husband's advancement to the Order of Deacon. I resolved to help him grow in the faith and to support his desire to serve the church in this sacred order. I made this request freely, motivated by no consideration other than the Glory of God.

I assist in a subliminal way in bringing the liturgical, pastoral, and charitable/social functions of his ministry to the people of God. Together, that adds a sense of God's calling for me in a lifelong, multifaceted service to his people. In short, I felt a "call" to serve also. Although I do believe that women could be deacons, I do not aspire to be a deacon. My "call" as a deacon's wife is a ministry just as spiritual.

The ministry of deacon's wife can be truly difficult, especially if you are a homemaker and mother of young children. The sacrifices are numerous. However, the spiritual growth this ministry provides lessens the stress and strain of daily living and instills a sense of acceptance of

God's will to serve, to be selfless. So, you take up your crosses, whatever they may be, and follow him. You submit and surrender all to God.

In the diaconate, the qualities of a deacon's wife are almost unlimited. She must be a prayerful individual. She must have felt the call to serve along with her husband. This call emphasizes a sense of oneness, as God has called us both through the sacrament of matrimony. She must be a peacemaker, a loving, affirming, patient, humble, forgiving woman, and a good listener. Yet she should have a sense of independence and individuality that nourishes her self-determination, sensitivity and courage to affect change and sets limits in their partnerships. Communication skills or any other God-given gifts are assets to this ministry. Most importantly, she must be serious and trustworthy.

As an extension of the deacon's ministry, the wife's responsibilities are just as great. Nevertheless, the "call" lifts the spirit higher in the soul. This ministry, in my case, almost comes naturally, as a result of my upbringing, my occupation and a vocation that extends to various pastoral functions: visiting the sick and shut-ins, teaching children and prisoners, leading small prayer and sharing groups, counseling those with problems. There are charitable and societal functions as well: helping and befriending the powerless who are in need, organizing and promoting community activities or programs to meet the special needs of unwed parents, caring for the needs of the elderly and disabled, visiting the lonely and neglected. Through these services, enlightened and informed by the spirit, "diakonia," or service of love, rises above the level of mere social service.

As I close, it is important to understand that the major responsibility of the deacon's wife in his ministry is that of working in harmony with all others in the parish church, especially its pastor, associate and other leaders, lending support wherever it is needed, while always building up the Body of Christ.

God has certainly called me to do his work, especially in our Afro-American community.

I have a tremendous concern for the small number of Afro-Americans in the diaconate program. However, I pray that God will touch the hearts, minds, bodies and souls of all men and women to revive, encourage and recognize the "call" to enter His vineyard, and in doing so, lift up the living spirit with perseverance and prayer.

I continue to thank God for the ability to be a part of the diaconate ministry as the wife of an Afro-American deacon.

6

The Deacon's Wife: A Personal Reflection

Maureen McGovern

A totally new dimension entered my life when, after 29 years of marriage, rearing six children and participating in civic and church community life, I learned that my husband, a Judge for the Commonwealth of Pennsylvania, was summoned by the Lord to ministry as Deacon. Following a period of formation and study lasting five years, one in which I fully participated, he was ordained in May, 1986. I share with you my thoughts garnered from the experience of living this new role in the work of the kingdom.

As a woman married to a man in Orders, I have had no particular problem retaining my own identity or self-image, in part because my husband and I have always managed both to share some interests and pursue others independently. He loves to garden and work out on Nautilus, but I do not; I enjoy choreographing and directing musicals, but he does not.

What I am most vigilant about as wife of a deacon is the perception others may have as to what my role as his wife should be. Since the Roman Catholic Church has no role models for married clergy, people tend to view the wife of a deacon in the old image of the Protestant minister's wife. She keeps the parish house clean, she meets with the women's club, she bakes the cookies for all the parish meetings, and she cooks dinner when the Bishop visits. I do none of the above.

My husband and I live in a parish with only one priest, the pastor, and 750 families with all the social problems our modern society has managed to produce. The opportunities for ministry, therefore, are endless. I myself function as Eucharistic Minister, Lector, teacher for the first and second grade sacramental program (we have no parish school), and member of both the Liturgy committee and the parish building committee. I also lead the rite for Distribution of Eucharist Outside of Mass when the pastor is not available for daily Mass. All of these activities preceded my husband's coming to Orders. My husband and I have organized the Aid for Friends Food Program, Ministers of Hospitality, and Eucharistic Ministers for the ill and home-bound.

In all of the above activities we see ourselves as facilitators, or enablers; we are there not to direct every detail but to coax and involve other members of the parish community to pick up the reins and drive on. We are there to encourage service. As soon as a particular ministry has been organized and a leader comes forward, I, or we, move on. We are blessed with a pastor who presents no obstacle to anything proposed for the parish so long as the project or program is well-organized and stays within the guidelines of the Church. There are currently over 200 people involved in some capacity in our parish. They need, and receive, from their clergy constant affirmation and support, and those of us in active ministries strive to support and affirm our clergy. Our deacon formation program at St. Charles Seminary afforded us rich experience in our faith life and education, but getting out there in the trenches with the people of God, both ordained and non-ordained, presents real challenges.

First, each of us in our community must be sacrament to each other. My husband and I are participants in sacrament by our witness, by our presence, and by our giving and receiving that which is part of every aspect of ordinary day-to-day living.

The second challenge is establishing a sense of collaboration, a synergy with all our co-workers. Neither my husband nor I are present in our parish in order to function apart from the community; we are there to support others in their ministries. Most rewarding in our ministry has been the happiness and dedication of those people who have become involved, who have consented to be led by the Spirit working in our community. There is no sense of a power struggle in our parish because all involved have a sense of being in this together, and we laugh at the good times and cry in the sad times, together.

The third challenge is to maintain an active prayer life. Try as we may, we are not going to satisfy every person's needs and hopes every single day. I keep reminding myself that nothing is perfect this side of heaven, and if Mrs. Smith does not care for the way some of our parishioners planted the tulip bulbs, I cannot change that. We are all human, God knows us better than we know ourselves, and we will have all the strength we need if we take the time to refresh ourselves in Eucharist and prayer.

I share in the Order of Deacon by virtue of the fact that it was conferred upon my husband. Our lives are conjoined in Matrimony and Orders, the diaconate is woven into the fabric of our married lives. I do not seek, nor have I ever sought, ordination for myself. I simply do not feel called to Orders. I can, however, as a woman and a mother, sometimes reach people when the ordained male cannot. My particular charisms and intuitions enable me to be present to others as Christ would have me be, in a way others cannot be, not because I am something special but because each of us is unique in what we bring to others as messengers of the Lord. It does, however, sadden me that our Church presently has no room for those women, wives of Deacons or otherwise, who are called to ministry as ordained Deacons. We are deprived of the unique dimensions they would offer to our communities, for example, as homilists or as presiders at Baptisms.

In the Apostolic Letter stating norms for the Order of Diaconate, the Deacon is referred to as a bridge between the "higher orders and the laity." I personally have a problem with this description; before Vatican II, people saw their church clearly separated into them (the clergy) and us (the people); but with today's tension between higher orders and laity, that Deacon-bridge would be swinging to and fro all the time. I prefer to think of all of us, ordained and laity, on the bridge together working and struggling to realize the kingdom both here and on the other side. This does not mean I reject the institutional Church, any more than I do the series of higher courts and jurists in my husband's profession. I simply feel that in the area of ministry in which all of us labor we must experience a commonality and relationship, and that comes to us through Baptism. Through Baptism we are church and our common labor is ministry.

I do not look to ordained clergy to lead me but to walk with me. We share different ministries, we each possess different gifts and charisms. I submit that until we learn to walk our journey hand in hand, learning from each other, leaning upon one another, our church is incomplete.

Daily I ask for the grace to be open to the unspoken call of those in need of love, those who are deeply wounded. I ask for a heart that is always open to support others with smiles and understanding and forgiveness, and I ask that the Lord will be my source of strength and understanding and peace as I open myself to all ministry asks of me.

7

Laying the Cornerstone for an Integral Ministry

John Williams

When I reflect upon my own experience of training with diaconal candidates and their wives in pastoral counseling here in the Diocese of La-Crosse, the one idea that hits me most deeply is that ordaining women to the diaconate is an idea whose time has come. This is the first and most important change I would propose for the upcoming 1990 Synod in Rome. Prior to the Synod, I would hope that such a change could be supported and introduced through a unanimous consensus of all the national episcopal conferences of the Americas.

Why an idea whose time has come? If someone were to have asked me to comment upon the suitability of the diaconal wives with whom I have worked in the Program for diaconal ministry, I could easily identify a majority of them as suited for this call, based upon their previous experience and preparation for ministerial work, their commitment to the Church, and their readiness. I do not know whether other faculty in the Program would agree with this because many of the women, especially in the first class we prepared, kept a low profile.

There were exceptions to this, of course. One of the women who was excited to be involved in the program found herself intimidated by the reactions she was getting to her participation because she seemed to be "upstaging" some of the men who were involved. She is simply a gifted leader and she stood out no more than some men who tended to take the lead in the training. Once the second group of candidates were in the program, and the women had become an integral part of the training, the diaconal wives showed strong evidence of their leadership qualities. In fact, at least four of the six were active leaders in their local parishes. One of the pastors from whose parish two of the couples came has recently authored a book on partnership in ministry; and I can remember how enthused he became as we reflected upon their qualifications.

Just thinking about his reaction brings me to a point that is crucial. I can imagine that, given the status of marriage and of relationships between men and women in New Testament times, the existence of ministerial couples like Aquila and Priscilla would have been something of a rarity. However, when I thought about the diaconal couples in our diocese, I can think of at least seven who could work better as a ministerial team than they are able to under the present solo arrangement. Some have been used to working as a team in such programs as the premarital program and Marriage Encounter.

However, I could see some expanded possibilities for team collaboration in the diaconate. An elderly couple might specialize in ministry to the aging or to shut-ins as a team. Another might specialize in ministry to the sick, while a third would devote themselves to youthwork. Such specialties are not the only way couples could minister pastorally. Collaborative ministry shared by couples has a variety of possibilities. At the same time, this type of sharing would often lend more, not less, balance to the marriage. Though the juggling of responsibilities can place a burden on the marriage, frequently two heads are better than one in the balancing effort. In the case of one diaconal couple in our diocese, the husband is quite involved in ministering to the sick, while his wife is partially disabled. Though it might not be physically possible for this couple to be involved in a team ministry to the sick or elderly at this point, their marriage would lend itself beautifully to such an enterprise of service. It would offer consolation along with a witness of love.

So far I have said little about the specific gifts that women would bring to service in the diaconal ministry. That is because I have been concentrating upon a major gift that most of them would identify first, I think, if

asked to identify their own qualifications: the sense and reality of their re-
latedness to their diaconal spouses, their churches, and the people they
serve. However, there are specific gifts these women possess. One is a
talented musician and leader in liturgy. Two others are adept as coun-
selors. Others have been involved in ministry to youth and adults. Among
these women are those who are serious about the contemplative life so
needed in the present age. Many are adept in identifying the needs of
others, a starting point in pastoral work. Most of all, these women are
deeply in tune with other women, and, in terms of active participation,
women today are the strength of the Church.

After many hours of talking to these women, I am convinced that they
would bring a different mindset to the ministry of preaching. In contrast to
a church which so often focuses the effect of sin back upon the sinner,
some show attunement to a sense of sin as victimization with ill effects
upon the persons sinned against. Some are wary of a type of preaching
that communicates to people the ulterior message that they can never do
enough for others. In a word, women would speak in different voices
about living the Christian life. One of the diaconal wives has told me that
she would like to write an article on "The Eighth Sorrow of Mary: Her
Grief over the Loss of Saint Joseph." Along with fresh and different
perspectives, women would bring to homiletics a different language.

For centuries, the Church has been represented by a ministry which
provides a presence at "half-mast," one which only partially corresponds to
the four marks of the Church. Just as the word "man" inadequately represents a humanity composed of both men and women, so also a male ministry cannot express the reality of a Church that is one, holy, and catholic.
Only an integral ministry can bear witness to the reality of a community in
which there is unity, solidarity, love, and inclusive justice, or at least a
human approximation to these characteristics. The ordination of women to
the diaconate would be equivalent to laying the cornerstone for the building of an integral ministry. There are lots of changes in the shape of ministry today that might quantitatively enhance the mission of the Church in
contemporary society; but I can think of none that would qualitatively so
change its composition, its mission, and its orientation to service for the
better as much as this one would.

8

A Brazilian View

Deacon Ademí Pereire de Abreu

In December of 1972, I was ordained to the permanent diaconate, and since retiring from my law practice in 1980 I have been a full-time deacon. Over the years I have served in several roles, as coordinator of the Archdiocesan Commission of Deacons for the state of Santa Catarina, as executive secretary of the Brazilian National Commission of Deacons, as Archdiocesan Coordinator of Extraordinary Ministers and, most recently, as a board member of the International Diaconate Center.

But from the time I was ordained I have had the chance to work directly with the People of God. So, now that our eight children are all graduated from college, my wife, Nagibe Cherem de Abreu, and I started to plan already in 1986 to free me from all these coordination activities, and in January of 1988 I took charge of the overall leadership of a small community with 1500 inhabitants out in the countryside of Ilha de Santa Catarina. We had bought a piece of property and built a house there, but only in October of 1988 were we able to move for good to Sao Joao de Rio Vermelho.

From what I have seen of our situation today in Brazil, the question of the diaconate for women is important from a pastoral perspective.

When our diocese of Florianopolis chose to go into the permanent diaconate, the aim was to have people in the communities on the outskirts of towns and in the rural areas who could stimulate the church communities toward growth in the gospel—in other words, to make them alive in faith, hope and *charity*. That happened in the late 1960s and early 1970s. Today we have 50 deacons, and almost all are working in communities with good results. We can say that the idea has worked out well.

But just in our diocese alone we have almost a thousand communities without deacons. Who keeps these communities alive? The answer is difficult: some are clearly in decline, others manage to get by with a visit from the priest-pastor every two weeks or every month, while others have lay leadership that keeps them alive and even growing.

Such lay leadership generally is supported by Extraordinary Ministers, almost half of whom are women. If around 60% of the Extraordinary Ministers are active, responsible and concerned about announcing the Good News, the percentage rises to 80% among women! In other words, in percentage terms, women are more effective and dedicated in the work of community leadership.

Some of these women are the *soul* of their communities and I believe that they could very well enter the diaconate training centers and, if confirmed in their vocation to *serve*, they could be ordained for diaconal ministry.

When this idea has come up in conversation with some bishops and priests, most of them have told me, "But these women are already doing everything: they reserve and distribute the eucharist, they administer the sacrament of baptism, they are authorized to witness marriages in the name of the Church. So why the diaconate? That would just be a formality."

It is precisely this narrowly immediate and utilitarian way of seeing things, keeping women out of the hierarchy and away from the sacrament of orders, that undermines the power of *sacramental grace* and makes these women feel that they are just being used and even regarded as "disposable material."

It is worth noting that this narrowly immediate and utilitarian idea has become so pervasive among our priests and bishops that in many dioceses the permanent (male!) diaconate is not accepted because people say "the extraordinary ministers do anything a deacon does and if something goes wrong they can easily be done away with."

This way of acting is *not Christian, not Catholic, not Pauline*, since St. Paul accepted the most diverse kinds of lay leadership and diaconate.

I sometimes think that the hierarchical Church believes in the ability and power of people, but no longer puts much faith in *divine grace* which broadens, strengthens, and sanctifies the activity of these people.

This mindset, so obstructive to the establishment of the permanent male diaconate, is completely closed when it comes to a women's diaconate. And yet late last year there was a national meeting of Sisters in the Brazilian North and Northeast who are running *parishes*!

I have noticed that the women's diaconate is well-received in university circles and among young people in the cities. In the countryside, in conservative dioceses, and even in dioceses that are otherwise progressive this idea is *anathema*. It is interesting to note that I have found the greatest number of female vocations to the diaconate in rural areas.

9

Pushing for the Diaconate for Women

Irene Löffler-Mayer

In the resolution on "Ministries and Offices" forwarded to Rome by the 1975 General Synod of the Dioceses of the Federal Republic of Germany, Votum 3 reads:

> to examine the question of the diaconate for women in accordance with contemporary theological understanding, and in view of the present pastoral situation to admit women to ordination to the diaconate if possible.

It was during my theology studies, as I was preparing a paper on the status of women in church and society, that I first came across this passage. I remember well the feeling of being suspended in midair between two worlds as I delved into this theme; my reading ranged from the extreme feminists like Susan Sontag and Simone de Beauvoir to Gertrud von le Fort. And often I was quite without hope when I saw how seldom we women are allowed to occupy the place in the Church which Jesus allocated to women in his society. Although Church statements—even *Mulieris Dignitatem*—emphasize over and over that women and men have the same dignity before God, we women nevertheless constantly experience being tolerated and welcomed only in serving roles.

This Votum of the General Synod filled me with hope. I imagined that a professional field in which I could contribute my gifts might open up for me. Yet the diaconate was and remains reserved for men, and today more than ever it seems that nothing changes; the discussion in this area has unfortunately turned to female acolytes, a question unworthy of our time and of a Church which takes a stand for human rights in the world.

I have worked as a religion teacher and, at the moment, am taking maternal leave and working on my doctoral dissertation. The diaconate has come up in, among other places, my canon law studies, and I studied theology along with deacons for several years. What makes me hope for this needed diaconate of women, however, arises not from my study of canon law or Catholic theology or from my contact with male deacons, but from my experiences in daily life.

When I see that women are active in hospital pastoral ministry but cannot dispense the sacraments of the dying, even though the particular woman, the particular man, desires the support of this woman in the hour of death, then I ask myself, where is our respect for the person—for the dying and for the consoling?

When I think of education, I see how the little boys become aware very early that they are somehow better than the little girls, and how this consciousness is encouraged by the Catholic Church as long as both girls and boys are not officially permitted to be acolytes, and as long as both women and men are not admitted to all ministries and offices in the Church.

I can remember a religion class in which I had the girls and boys look for passages in the Old Testament which would show the feminine aspects of God, for example, God as a nursing mother. The students would not believe that God was spoken of and can be spoken of also in maternal-feminine images. Their image of God is purely masculine. Similarly, my experiences with female and male students during the discussion of the creation stories show how unfamiliar they are with the story in which woman and man are created according to the divine image, but how familiar with the creation of woman from the man's rib and its conventional degrading interpretation.

Am I digressing? What I consider essential is this: In calling upon tradition in the question of office, the Church is taking tradition seriously.

It is, however, not taking seriously the many women who today and throughout the history of Christendom have lived out their faith. The saying that "Anyone who loves the Church will be made to suffer" is certainly true for all Christians, but it is especially true for the women who are conscious that they, like the men, are created in the image of God, and who take this as their mandate. I know that those who have the say in the Church are for the most part men, but they know as well as I do that those who hand on the faith to the next generation are women. Many women in my circle of acquaintances, whether educated theologically or not, have gone into exile from the Church. They leave, they no longer find there the homeland they desire for themselves and their children.

It is my hope that my daughter will learn to know God in many dimensions, not only the exclusively masculine, and will have more opportunity than I to follow the call of God in this Church.

Many women still remain silent in the Church because they hope that in this feminine way, through service and sacrifice, they can attain equality in the Church through the back door. We let ourselves say that we have no right to demand the diaconate for women, that the time is not yet ripe. Yet if we continue to be silent, to hold back, to wait until being taken seriously as human beings in the Church is finally handed to us as a gift, then it is quite possible that we are ignoring God's mandate to us.

I am not consoled by the fact that the Church has had saints throughout the ages, and that sanctity need have nothing to do with ordination. How much have even the women who are placed before us as luminous models, like Edith Stein or Teresa of Avila, suffered from the fact that they as women counted for less than men—even if they fulfilled their roles more uncritically than we do!

10

Reflections from Praxis

Rita Gäng

The theme of "Women and Church" is once again awakening fresh public interest in the German Federal Republic and beyond. Even within the Church, the analyses and prognoses put forth by secular society are no longer taboo, for there have been recent papal statements.

In their September 1981 pastoral statement, "On Questions of the Place of Women in Church and Society," the German bishops spoke of a "challenge to our time and faith." In their introduction, the bishops say that the Church's confrontation with these questions is a matter not merely of such personal fundamental rights as human dignity and equality but also of the "common responsibility for the future of a more humane world."

In conclusion, they call upon all women "to recognize all the new possibilities for collaboration and co-responsibility in Church and society." As their most significant task, women should commit themselves both to the renewal and the humanization of society and also to assuring that the faithful can once again discover the true countenance of the Church. From my 20 years of service as a pastoral assistant (*Gemeindereferentin*), and thus as a full-time professional woman in the Church, I want to add to these extremely heartening statements of the German bishops two experiences of my own, and then to pose some questions.

First Example from Praxis

The usual way in which full-time professional colleagues in the Church relate to one another is still molded predominantly by male-oriented and at best task-related structures. Question: how can we—women and men—achieve a reversal in our own sector of the Church, so that the Divine Wisdom once again becomes determinative and supportive of human life both for individuals and for the formation of their community? Here we are concerned immediately and directly with the order of divine creation, in which it is not people's status that counts, but their animating membership in Jesus Christ: "There are no more distinctions between Jew and Greek, slave and free, male and female, but all of you are one in Jesus Christ" (Gal. 3:28). My own attempt to conform my life and professional identity in this way can, I hope, be demonstrated by the following example of a professional conference. From this praxis-experience I want to show that even within our hierarchical leadership structures it is possible to work as partners to form a unit of interpersonal relationship. Assuming, of course, that those involved venture together on the path of learning!

My current position is in a parish of 7000 Catholics in a town near Heidelberg. The parish leadership team is made up of the pastor, a part-time deacon, two secretaries, and myself, a full-time pastoral assistant. The weekly "conference" I am speaking of, however, includes only the pastor and myself and lasts an hour or two. During this time we are not disturbed by the telephone or other outside demands. The second part of the conference always focuses on pastoral tasks. But here I want to speak of my experiences of the first part. At the very beginning of my work here, we agreed on a regular conference. We proceed on the understanding that either of us may address or express any impressions or occurrences in the area of human relationships. In this way, our knowledge of one another's life history, along with mutual trust, grows in small cautious steps. In this context, too, "spiritual impulses" and contributions to our own personal spiritual life experience arise. Right now we are reading excerpts from a book about events in a parish which deliberately envisaged its own path of faith in terms of personal vocation. Such stories encourage us both! I don't want to gloss over the fact that these exchanges do not always go smoothly but occasionally strain our tolerance of both our own and other people's viewpoints and limits. What is important is weaning oneself from judging differences; this can, in fact, be learned. It can lead to a new esteem for the other and can advance one's own self-improvement.

What might this mean for an ordained diaconate for women? Through these conferences I myself can shape my own responsibilities in the practical pastoral leadership ministry of the parish. This perception has become increasingly clearer to me in the course of my professional years! It is nevertheless a fact that, although I understand the reception of the official diaconal ordination to be sufficiently justified on the one hand by my personal way of life and on the other by my pastoral activity, I do not want to seek it in the present church. My position is based primarily on two realities which I feel are linked: 1) the centralized church structure, which is growing still narrower, and 2) the failure of the official church to recognize the fully-human saving reality of man and woman in the biblical perspective based in the triune God.

My question is, what concrete changes are needed before a dynamic relationship between humans and God can once again find its birthright within the official church landscape?

Second Example from Praxis

Parallel to the hierarchical power structure "from above to below," most parishes are dominated by a largely unconscious tradition of a "pastoral principle of care and instruction" which keeps people immature. The resulting dependence of the parish on individual officeholders is in clear contradiction to the call to conversion of the 1975 synod of German dioceses, which called for seeking ways "to move away from a providing church and toward a mutually supportive grassroots church." We need to create a grassroots awareness and a fundamental human feeling which brings all the members of a Christian parish joy in their own growth, instead of fostering a passive submissiveness.

What might this mean for the official ordination of women to the diaconate? Parish life calls for a dynamic pastoral principle which defines itself from the "divine life-principle," from Spirit and Wisdom. Parochial faith develops according to the law of receiving and growing. The hidden aspects—as in the parable of the mustard seed—must not be overlooked.

To prepare the way for the diaconal office for women, in my opinion, we need to turn away from self-righteousness and to turn toward the one true God who is the shepherd of all people. This conversion, which must involve all members of the Church and come from within and from below, is not yet visible. In this connection, Ezekiel 34, "The bad shepherds of Israel," provides direction for us. In this changed climate, sister/brotherhood would have a good chance of success. The ministering faith-witness of Christian communities in their imitation of Jesus could increase its social impact.

My question is, how, concretely, do we arrive at such a fundamental reversal?

Guideposts for the Future

As we move along the path of learning how to deal sympathetically with one another as church people oriented to biblical partnership, we need imagination to plan for our future steps and caution in handing on the conventional understanding of human development. For the present, in the here and now, we should give a sisterly-brotherly kind of relationship precedence over all others. In this way, each of us can begin immediately where we are!

With the promise of Ezekiel 36:26, "I will give you a new heart and lay my spirit in you," God's action becomes visible as the most important pastoral.

A concluding remark: Perhaps one day, in a Third Vatican Council, it can be said of today's often tiring women's movement that it represented a "going through" of the Spirit of God, the *Ruach* of Yahweh.

11

Pursuing Our History

Ilse Schüllner

For me it all began more than 20 years ago when I completed my theological studies. My husband and I both felt ourselves called to the diaconate. The Second Vatican Council had made it possible for my husband to become a deacon, but I as a woman could not be ordained. So my husband became a deacon without the theological training and I was a theologian without ordination, although I too wanted to place my life entirely in the service of God and the Church and to form myself accordingly.

In the beginning my family duties, especially being with my own daughter, took up a good deal of my time. But today I am a grandmother and only occasionally care for my grandchildren.

My work in my school—I teach religion, sports, and mathematics in a Gymnasium, a university prep school—I would not want to give up even today. The real focal point for me is the religious education. Often it is the last contact our young people have with the Church. I attempt to dismantle their aggressions against the Church and to mediate to them, as well as I can, the loving nearness of God. It has always been a joy for me to teach and to participate in the students' questions and problems. I see this as part of my diaconal service.

In my parish, I dedicate myself to serious work with the mentally handicapped. A comparatively large number of these people live in the parish because there is a home for the handicapped in the area. I pick up a group for Mass on Sundays, talk with many of them, hold confirmation classes, arrange an afternoon meeting with a few young people, and reach out to individual mentally handicapped people at other times as well. I have found contact with these people a great enrichment, and learned and received much from them. Many have no contact with other people outside the home; more than half of the people living there even spend their Christmas in the home. I try to awaken interest in my parish for such contacts.

For some time I have been collaborating in an independent feminist seminar in the Theology Department of the University of Freiburg im Breisgau. This seminar has certainly made me still more sensitive to the concerns of women in the Church.

My membership on the editorial committee of the magazine *Diaconia XP* makes it possible for me to voice women's concerns in planning, in the teamwork, and in individual articles and meditations.

For 20 years now I have not ceased to continue working and fighting for the diaconate for women. When the International Diaconate Center (IDZ) was established here in Freiburg immediately after the Second Vatican Council, I was involved in the founding meeting. There had been efforts to introduce the diaconate for women already before Vatican II, so that even Cardinal Bea was of the opinion that the diaconate was more likely to be introduced for women than for men. We have continued these early efforts. The IDZ considered the diaconate for women so important that a seat on the board was provided specifically for this dimension. At the 1973 IDZ conference in Innsbruck, I was chosen for this position, and ever since I have worked to fulfill that task to the best of my abilities and powers.

Because the origin of the diaconate is traced back to Acts 6:1-7, and that same passage was cited in the reintroduction of the diaconate for males, I found myself moved to examine it in the original Greek text. What I discovered was that this probably represents the first exclusion of women from the beginnings of an "official" ministry. I would like to sketch the most important aspects of my reflections here.

The usual translation of Acts 6:1 reads something like this: "About this time, when the number of disciples was increasing, the Hellenists made a complaint against the Hebrews: in the daily distribution their own widows were being overlooked" (Jerusalem Bible). The solution to the problem follows: through the mediation of the apostles, the seven are installed. The scene is explained by all the commentaries as the feeding of the Hellenistic widows, as care for the poor.

The first question which occurred to me was, Why does it say only "widows" and not "widows and orphans," the customary Old Testament expression for such needy groups? And then there surely must have been other poor people around—what of them? Why only widows, and then only the widows of the Hellenists? Who were the Hebrews, who were the Hellenists, and to which group did the apostles belong? Were there still other groups?

I turned to the original Greek text to find an answer. There, to my amazement, I found the following, which I translate literally: ". . . there arose a murmur of the Hellenists against the Hebrews, because disdained (or more rarely, overlooked) were in ministry (*diakonia*) daily their widows." The word *diakonia* originally referred to service or ministry at the table, but it is always used in an active way, in the sense of performance of service rather than the service rendered. Luke uses the word *diakonia* eight more times in Acts, and always in the primary sense: service of the word (6:4), ministry entrusted by Jesus (20:24), service in Jerusalem (12:25), ministry among the pagans (21:19), sharing in the same ministry (1:17), taking over this ministry and apostolate (1:25). Only once is it used in the sense of collective assistance (11:29), but here too it is used in an active sense, being dispensed by the disciples.

The other writings of the New Testament are no different in the way they use this term. So our passage can be translated in the same way to read that in the daily ministry they performed, the widows of the Hellenists were held in contempt by the Hebrews. Now the text has a completely different meaning. The widows had cooperated in preparing and carrying out the daily agape celebration. Earlier Acts 2:46-47 had said, "They went as a body to the Temple every day but met in their houses for the breaking of bread; they shared their food gladly and generously."

This new translation is further supported by what follows. According to 6:3, the apostles had been participating in the work of the festive meal, for the text says, "We (the apostles) will hand over this duty to them, and continue to devote ourselves to prayer and to the service of the word."

If the translation and explanation which has been current until now—that the support of the widows was being overlooked, and that the apostles were serving at table—is adhered to, then the onus of negligence falls entirely upon the apostles. But the text contains no such reproach, and in fact it is hard to imagine such a thing when it is precisely these apostles who undertake to mediate between the two groups.

So the two smaller groups of Hebrews and Hellenists must have existed within the larger group of Christians. The apostles and many of the disciples—male and female—certainly spoke Aramaic as a rule and were not necessarily included among either the Hellenists or the Hebrews. That much has been accepted without question until now.

It is, then, quite plausible that these widows were not in need of care, but rather were being denied their active ministry. When the attitude of the Hebrews toward women ministering evoked rather serious tensions in the community, the apostles conducted an election and commissioned the seven by the laying on of hands. Some exegetes see in this a regular ordination rite. The apostles themselves withdrew from this more liturgical ministry in order to proclaim the word of God. The women are not mentioned again; either they were limited to subordinate, practical preparatory service without serving at table, or they were excluded completely. Either, according to my thesis, would involve the handing down of the first exclusion of women from office!

How did the understanding of this passage come to be limited to the one interpretation? Not a single exegete until now has considered the alternative presented here, even though use of the word *diakonia* in such a passive sense would be unique, and a more solidly-based translation is available: "were despised in their daily ministry" rather than "were being overlooked in the daily distribution." The only explanation I find is that all the exegetes simply accepted as obvious the idea that widows were poor and needed to be cared for. This pre-understanding has been stronger than the knowledge that in the Jerusalem congregation almost everything was shared.

This is just one of the many aspects of the whole tradition on women in the Church which must be reconsidered—the patriarchal character of the Church, its masculine style, its exclusion of women's voices.

In November of 1981, our German bishops stated that the matter of the diaconal office for women needs ongoing discussion and a more general agreement within the entire Church before further steps can be undertaken. Ten years ago, the national synods of Germany, the Netherlands, Austria and Switzerland had already requested the diaconate for women. In Switzerland, no deacons were to be ordained until women too were admitted to this office; that resolution was not adhered to. Many bishops around the world have spoken out in favor of women deacons. At the grassroots, where discussion on the place of women is always going on, the diaconate is desired. We German women experience great support from some of the male deacons. But we are also pained that a goodly number of German deacons do oppose the diaconate for women, no doubt seeing in it a personal threat to their own understanding of their role. On the whole, however, it must be said that the broad support called for by the bishops does in fact exist, and it is urgent and necessary that women be admitted to the office of deacon.*

---

*Note: Frau Schüllner's research is developed more fully in the September, 1989, issue of *Diaconie XP*.

12

On Fighting Gently But Consistently

Barbara Sequeira

I am Barbara Sequeira, lover of God the Creator, follower of Jesus the Redeemer, and empowered by the Holy Spirit. I feel called to serve the Church in a deeper way than I am presently given permission to do. I came to this calling slowly over many years of learning and growing in my faith. My story begins early in my life. I was raised in a matriarchal family. My father was a strong "church" person involved as much as a layman could be at that time. My mother and grandmother both "left the Church" over the birth control issue, although the issue was much broader for my mother. She recognized that the male hierarchical structure excludes women from main functionary and decision-making roles in the Church.

My reaction as a young adult to this family diversity was to follow and believe strongly in the "Church" and to marry a man who was much like my father in his love and involvement in the Church. My education had included CCD training from the first grade to the eighth and some Catholic club involvement in high school and college. I also attended a small liberal arts Catholic women's college in Marin County in California for two years.

My spiritual awakening came in bits and pieces. Confirmation was an important experience for me, and I truly began to see Christ as a part of my life. My faith became more alive to me when I dated and married my husband, John. He taught me so much about what living my faith meant. I envied his education in theology and church. He was raised with an all-Catholic education, grammar school through college. In the early years of our marriage and the period of having and raising a family, I grew in my desire to serve the people of God. While living in Reno, Nevada, I took a CCD teacher training course that introduced me to the changes of Vatican II. This was in 1967-68. I took another class in Los Angeles when we moved there in 1971. My excitement grew at the changes in the liturgy, the thinking, and the return to gospel teachings. John and I went on a Marriage Encounter and I saw our sacrament in a whole new light. Our love for one another could make a difference in our own lives and in others'. We are a "little church"—We are the church!

My excitement continued until John was asked to bring the Eucharist to the sick and I was told I was to wait in the car and not to go into the house. This was the order of the pastor of the parish, standard in 1975 in Los Angeles. When we moved back to the San Francisco Bay area, where John had been born and raised, I decided to return to college and get a California teaching credential. After I accomplished that, including student teaching at the age of 39, I could not find a job teaching social studies. God called me in a new way, through a friend who suggested I get a master's degree in Religious Studies. I accomplished this in just over a year and started teaching at a Catholic girls' high school in the town in which we lived. Then, and only then, was I asked to be a lector and later a Eucharistic minister. My husband, of course, had continued his lectoring and ministering. I was thrilled at serving in this way, but there were always the odd glances, the line of communicants that would not come to me, the letters to the pastor about women on the altar. It was at this period that I saw myself in a new light. I began to see that I could do more and should do more to serve.

My teaching of young women has led me to listening and caring, and loving these girls. They see me on the altar willing to serve in any and all ways—I am and want to be a role model for them. I want to be that and much more to the whole church.

John first heard of the permanent diaconate in Los Angeles. Then it was only for men with grown children, so he waited. Then he inquired again in our parish in the San Francisco area. When the program was announced, the pastor put John's name in as a candidate. During the discernment process, I was asked my opinion of his being a deacon, but other than this token acknowledgement, I was never much involved.

During the three years that we have been in the program, I have felt more and more strongly that this is where I could serve the best. I have done the same work, papers, classes, Saturday workshops, and ministry that my husband has done. I will continue to learn all that these classes offer, despite the fact that much of the material I had already studied in my master's program. I see the diaconate as a service to the church that is imperative. Married people, working for a living, raising a family, constantly involved with people with real-world problems and struggling with those problems themselves, can bring so much to the people of God. We are not removed from society, put in a seminary and then set up in a rectory to do our job. We perform our jobs and live out our roles while living life with its joys and struggles, loving each other and our children, and then extending that love to the people of God. There is nothing unique in John's maleness that allows him to serve better than I could. If anything, the qualities of a woman like myself are what ministry is all about—caring, lifegiving, gentle, spiritual, nurturing. Just think how powerful ministry could be if we combined the male strength and objectivity with these "feminine" qualities!

I see the diaconate as not only serving but nurturing the people of God, who in turn can go out and minister to one another. As the priest feeds and nourishes his community, so does the deacon. I see myself clearly in that role and feel strongly called to it.

I talk much about this struggle and desire within me. I am received with joy and awe by some, but I am put down at every turn by anyone higher in the hierarchy than my pastor. I am indeed fortunate to be in a parish that allows me to participate fully in ministry and even evaluates me along with my husband. It supports my desires and talents for the church. John is a great support. He would love to see any woman who has gone through the formation, participated fully, and has the desire to be ordained, ordained along with any man with the same qualifications.

The diaconate formation group that John and I are in is very special. The first time a photographer wanted to take a picture of just the candidates, they refused and said we are all candidates. In this group, we seldom hear anything like "I am here only to support my husband." We are more likely to hear that the woman is there for her own growth. Even the women who do not do the paperwork and classwork are involved in some kind of ministry.

Two of the candidates' wives, myself being one of them, and one of our spiritual directors flew back to Washington, D.C. in October of 1987 to the Women in the Church Conference. We heard Sandra Schneiders, among many others who believe as we do, tell us not to change patriarchy for matriarchy but to create a community in which all people are allowed and encouraged to dialogue and give input. We three women brought the Sandra Schneiders' video tape back and showed it to the deacon candidates and their wives. Then we shared our own stories. The men were beautiful—they cried for us and hugged us.

The following year, John was motivated enough to attend the Future of the American Church Conference with me. He gained an even broader perspective, and he shares these ideas with his associates in the diaconate and in business. This is one way I see change coming about.

I love the Church that I grew up in, yet it is painful to participate in a body that I believe ignores the Gospel message in many of its decisions. The hurt goes on. The struggle goes on. I will stay in and fight gently and consistently.

13

The Minnesota Experience

Maria Hill, C.S.J.
Phyllis A. Willerscheidt

The Commission on Women of the Archdiocese of St. Paul and Minneapolis began discussing the issue of women becoming deacons at a brainstorming session in 1979. The concept was then brought up again at a regional conference on the Role of Women in the Church in Alexandria, Minnesota, in September of 1982. Again at a conference in 1984, "Women and Men Relating," the issue was raised, but no action was taken at that time because the Bishops in the United States were not open to such deliberations.

During the listening sessions in the Fall of 1984, the concept of the permanent diaconate surfaced in several of the sessions. When the topic was again discussed in 1987 by the Commission on Women, some of the members of the Commission were opposed to the idea. One member stated to the assembly, "If the women suffragettes continued to discuss like this, we still wouldn't have the vote." The Commission on Women took the suggestion to Archbishop Roach at the annual meeting on January 14, 1987. His immediate response was to go ahead and study and work at it, for "it is potentially achievable."

Beginning in February of 1987, the Permanent Diaconate Task Force of the Commission on Women met monthly to study the ordination of women to the permanent diaconate and to make a recommendation to Archbishop

Roach regarding their research. An initial brainstorming session elicited ten areas for research:

1. History of the diaconate program in the Western Church;
2. Experiences of non-Anglo deacons in the diaconate;
3. Preparation for becoming a deacon: admission/course work/testing/evaluations;
4. The realities of becoming a deacon: overview/time/ duties/salary;
5. Diaconate programs around the United States: numbers/ different duties/salary/survey possibilities;
6. Diaconate programs around the world;
7. Papal and Church writings on the Diaconate;
8. Popular writings on the diaconate, including a clipping service;
9. Involvement of unmarried women/married women;
10. Open Forum programs, as needed for input.

Efforts to develop the research continued on numbers 1, 3, 4, 6, and 7; the committee did some minor study on 2, 8, and 9, and did not follow up on number 5 except to make contacts with other women in the United States who had discussed the subject.

During succeeding meetings, the committee read and discussed numerous articles, position papers, and books. A variety of individuals were invited to speak to the group, including:

- a director of the Permanent Diaconate
- a faculty member for the Permanent Diaconate
- a member of the Curriculum subcommittee
- wives of permanent deacons

One member attended a provincial deacons' conference in St. Cloud, Minnesota. The group contacted other dioceses interested in the diaconate for women to discover what was happening around the country. In March of 1985, a task force of the Milwaukee Archdiocese's Commission on Women wrote a paper on the position of admitting women to the diaconate. As far as it can be determined, there was no follow-up to that paper. We also learned that a statement has been sent annually from Chicago to the Sacred Congregation in Rome, via the National Catholic Conference of Bishops, requesting a program to look into ordaining women to the permanent diaconate. There has never been a response to this effort.

Three basic assumptions focused the study for the group:

1. Some women feel called to the Diaconate and have the gift of service to the Church.

2. There is nothing in Scripture or tradition that prevents women from being deacons. In fact, Scripture confirms that there were women deacons in the early Church.

3. The Church would be enriched by extending the Diaconate to women.

From the information gleaned through our research and discussion, an outline for a position paper was developed. Each task force member was made responsible for reviewing the material and developing a first draft of one section. At each succeeding meeting, the drafts were reviewed by the committee. Suggestions were made and the task force members incorporated them into the next draft.

Throughout the process the group kept in touch with national and international developments in the areas of the role of women in ministry and the permanent diaconate, networking with other interested persons and reading current resources. This new information gave impetus to the task force discussions and provided fresh insights for writing the document.

Reader teams will review the document. After these suggestions have been integrated into the position paper, it will be offered to the Commission on Women for approval. At that point, the paper will be submitted in the form of a recommendation to Archbishop Roach.

Concomitant with the study of the permanent diaconate for women were the feedback sessions on the first draft of the United States Bishops' pastoral on women. All of the task force members were involved in those sessions, planning and facilitating them, participating in the discussions, collating the responses, and writing the summary which was submitted to the Bishops.

In considering the role of women in the Church, it is difficult to ignore the permanent diaconate for women. The response to the pastoral shows clear support for a study of the permanent diaconate for women to be completed soon. The majority of persons who attended the eight feedback sessions in this Archdiocese shared similar views.

A special concern of the task force has been the whole issue of inclusive language. The manner in which language shapes our view of reality is an important one. Reality consists of how we see things in our world, not only objects but values, attitudes, stereotypes and feelings. We use words and symbols to describe our world. What happens when someone is not mentioned at all, such as in gender-exclusive language? Girls and women are often excluded from images that reflect their reality.

When God is considered only in male terms, there is no room for female images. The use of human terms to describe God is inappropriate as well, because this, too, limits God. However, in the current patriarchal system in this country and in the Church, it appears that continuing to use male terms to describe God values men and devalues women.

Similarly, when one thinks of deacons only in male terms, one loses sight of female images performing ministerial roles. *Diakonia* means service. Although women have been socialized to serve and nurture others from early childhood, their gifts are not being fully utilized under the current Church structure.

In the beginning, some members of the Commission on Women believed the diaconate for women would never become a reality and did not want to waste time researching the issue. They felt present hierarchical Church structure would not permit open dialogue on the topic. Other women argue that ordaining women as deacons would only prevent the possibility of ordaining women as priests. The biggest obstacle encountered in the process of writing the position paper was the sheer volume of related material to review and digest. An intelligent study of the possibility of the ordination of women to the permanent diaconate demands a broad study of scripture, Church history and Church documents. The vastness of the project was revealed only after the group was well into the project. The task force anticipated completing the work by December of 1987. However, at the time of this writing (June, 1989) the task has still not been completed, even though the group is working diligently toward conclusion of the project.

While there are many scriptural and historical references, the current material on women and the permanent diaconate is scarce. The Commission has felt virtually alone in the search for support in this effort.

In conclusion, the Commission on Women has been mindful of the 1979 statement of the Minnesota Bishops: "A woman who views herself as the image of God is conscious of her great dignity, a dignity which bestows self-acceptance and self-esteem. Holding this God-view toward herself and towards other women, she is called to extend this recognition outward to all people, enabling all to value and enhance each other's dignity as responsible and loving persons. Wherever, within the Church or society, a woman does not find liturgies, educational programs, social events or decision-making structures which meet her own and others' needs, she should work with persistence to establish them."

Thus, the Commission on Women has given itself a mandate to work tirelessly to pursue issues of justice for women within the Archdiocese of St. Paul and Minneapolis. One of these efforts is the research project on the diaconate for women and active support of its recommendations.

14

Women Deacons: Some Historical Highlights

Arlene Swidler

Our history of women deacons must begin with two references from the beginnings of Christianity itself, the New Testament. In both cases we find women associated with the diaconate, but in neither case are we sure precisely what that role involves.

In Romans 16:1 (written about 55 A.D.) Paul refers to Phoebe as a *diakonos* of the church at Cenchreae, the port city of Corinth. That word *diakonos*—literally, deacon—gets translated into English in various ways. Some translations avoid having to give her a title at all by changing the sentence structure. The Good News Bible says, "Phoebe, who serves the church at Cenchreae," and Monsignor Knox, in his translation, says, "she has devoted her services to the Church at Cenchreae." In other translations, such as the Revised Standard Edition, the New American Bible and the Jerusalem Bible, she is simply referred to as a "deaconess." This is somewhat misleading. The Greek word used to describe Phoebe is the masculine *diakonos*, not the feminine form, *diakonissa*, which came into existence only later, when the differing liturgical roles for the two sexes were carefully defined and it was therefore important to distinguish between the women and the men.

Precisely what Phoebe did as a deacon we don't know. We do know that she was included in the biblical understanding of diaconate or ministry. She is venerated by the Orthodox Church as St. Phoebe, the first of the deaconess-saints.

The second pertinent passage comes from I Timothy 3:8-12 (date and authorship uncertain—probably about 125 A.D.). "Deacons likewise must be serious, not double-tongued, not addicted to much wine, not greedy for grain; they must hold the mystery of the faith with a clear conscience. And let them also be tested first; then if they prove themselves blameless, let them serve as deacons. *The women likewise must be serious, no slanderers, but temperate, faithful in all things.* Let deacons be married only once, and let them manage their children and their households well . . . ." (RSV translation; our italics)

Just who are "the women" referred to here? Because the statement is situated right in the middle of a passage on deacons, it can not refer to Christian women in general. It has occasionally been argued that the women referred to are the wives of deacons, but the fact that in the parallel preceding passage (vv.1-7), which deals with bishops, there are no directives for their wives makes that argument unconvincing. So we are left to believe that these are women who have a specific role, a certain function which is similar to that of the male deacons.

What we get from the New Testament sources, then, is first, that women were referred to as deacons, and second, that women most probably performed ministries similar to those of male deacons. These women deacons were recognized outside the Christian community as well. Pliny the Younger, writing about the year 111 from Asia Minor to the Roman Emperor Trajan, speaks of the torture of two women servants (*ancillae*) who were called deacons (*ministrae,* in Latin).

Later on, some of the early Fathers of the Church taught that the women referred to in the New Testament were actually deacons in an official sense. This is more than most people would claim today.

Origen (third century), for example, believed that Phoebe was installed as a deacon. In his Commentary on Romans 10:17 he says, "This text (Rom 16:1-2) teaches with the authority of the Apostle that even women are instituted deacons in the Church. This was the function which was exercised in the Church of Cenchreae by Phoebe, who was the object of high praise and recommendation by Paul." St. John Chrysostom (fourth century), in his Homily XXX on the Epistle to the Romans, says, "See how many ways he takes to give her dignity. For he has both mentioned her before all the rest, and called her sister. And it is no slight thing to be called the sister of Paul. Moreover he has added to her rank, by mentioning her being a 'deacon.' "

Chrysostom also believed that the women referred to in the passage from the Letter to Timothy were themselves deacons. "Some have thought that this is said of women generally, but it is not so, for why should he introduce anything about women to interfere with his subject? He is speaking of those who hold the rank of deacons."

Women probably began to be referred to as "deaconesses" when a special order of deaconesses was founded. At that point, it was no longer simply a matter of helping and ministering to people privately and unofficially, but of being officially designated and receiving one of the minor orders, at least. For several centuries the order of deaconesses flourished, then it slowly faded away around the sixth century in the Western Church. Within that time and from place to place, the role and understanding of the deaconess varied.

Such diversity is not surprising. Male offices in the New Testament and the early Church were also fluid, and even today different churches interpret the tradition in different ways. Some churches have bishops, some don't. Some have deacons, some don't. Some have presbyters or priests, some don't. Early Church history does not provide us with a neat formula.

The old documents from these early centuries do present a number of interesting facts. First of all, the deaconesses were considered clerics. The Council of Nicaea (325) refers to them as clerics. And the Council of Chalcedon (451) speaks of the ordination of both deacons and deaconesses with the laying on of hands. These were both ecumenical councils, universal in jurisdiction. On the other hand, some local councils—always Western—were more negative. The Council of Nimes in France (394) said women should not be a part of the clergy, and the Council of Orange, also in France (441), forbade ordaining deaconesses.

A good source of information on the early office of the deaconess is the Apostolic Constitutions, which, despite its name, is a document from the fourth century. It is a collection of liturgical and canonical documents which includes and expands on earlier materials such as the Didascalia, Didache, writings of Hippolytus, and canons from the Councils of Antioch and Laodicea.

Here we learn that the deaconess had a role quite different from that of the male deacon, and quite subordinate. She was not to "do or say anything without the deacon." In the lists of clerics, deaconesses follow deacons. "A deaconess does not bless, nor perform anything belonging to the office of presbyters or deacons, but is only to keep the doors, and to minister to the presbyters in the baptizing of women, on account of decency."

From early sources we learn that deaconesses were educated sufficiently to instruct women before baptism, that they were intermediaries between the clergy and women, that they distributed communion to the women and children, visited women in their homes, and administered the sacrament of the Anointing of the Sick to women. They welcomed women to the liturgical assemblies and accompanied women who were meeting with the deacon or bishop. They were also entrusted with carrying messages, even long distances.

The deaconess was held in great honor. "Let also the deaconess be honored by you in place of the Holy Ghost. . . . And as we cannot believe in Christ without the teaching of the Spirit, so let not any woman address herself to the deacon or bishop without the deaconess."

Probably the single most important task of the deaconess was to anoint the women's bodies at baptism after the deacon had anointed their foreheads. At this time, baptism was by immersion. After the bishop anoints those to be baptized and immerses them, says the Apostolic Constitutions, "let a deacon receive the man and a deaconess the woman, that so the conferring of this inviolable seal may take place with a becoming decency." As the church custom moved from adult baptism to infant baptism, the need for this service vanished, followed by the order of deaconess.

* * * * *

Interest in reviving the order of deaconesses arose in both the Protestant and the Eastern Orthodox Churches in the second half of the last century. In Russia, the reactivation was first proposed by the Grand Duchess Elena Pavlovna, and the effort continued with help from bishops and women. In modern Greece, women have actually been ordained as deaconesses. In 1911, St. Naktarios ordained a woman with the same ritual used for the ordination of a male deacon, and since then nuns have been ordained as deaconesses in other Greek monasteries; when no ordained clergymen are present, they read the gospel during Divine Service, and they bring communion to all nuns who are ill.

The issue continues to be discussed. In late 1988, an Inter-Orthodox Theological Consultation on Women in the Church convened in Chambésy, Switzerland. The 14 autonomous Orthodox Churches sent official delegates, and close to 50 other theologians attended. Eighteen of the participants were women. Although the consultation spoke of "the impossibility of ordination of women to the special priesthood" for traditional reasons, it clearly favored ordaining women to the diaconate.

> The apostolic order of deaconesses should be revived. It was never altogether abandoned in the Orthodox Church, though it had tended to fall into disuse. There is ample evidence, from apostolic times, from the patristic, canonical and liturgical tradition, well into the Byzantine period (and even in our own day) that this order was held in high honor . . . .

> Such a revival would represent a positive response to many of the needs and demands of the contemporary world in many spheres. This would be all the more true if the Diaconate in general (male as well as female), were restored in all places in its original, manifold services (*diakoniai*), with extension in the social sphere, in the spirit of ancient tradition and in response to the increasing specific needs of our time. It should not be solely restricted to a purely liturgical role or considered to be a mere step on the way to higher "ranks" of clergy.

The revival of women deacons in the Orthodox Church would emphasize in a special way the dignity of women and give recognition to her contribution to the work of the Church as a whole.

The deaconesses we are familiar with today in many of the other Christian churches trace their history back to the work of Theodor Fliedner of Kaiserswerth, Germany, who founded the modern Protestant order of deaconesses in 1836 with the entrance of his first recruit, 48-year-old Gertrud Reichardt. Protestant deaconesses were not unknown at that time. Fliedner himself had seen the work of the Anabaptist and Mennonite deaconesses in the Netherlands. Earlier, in the Massachusetts Bay Colony, Governor William Bradford had written of a deaconess who ministered to the sick and poor and during religious meetings sat "with a little birchen rod in her hand, and kept little children in great awe from disturbing the congregation"—preserving order in the women's section of a liturgical assembly had been the task of the deaconess from the beginning.

Nevertheless, it was Pastor Fliedner's work in founding an order of deaconesses that began a whole movement. Fliedner was trained and ordained as a Lutheran. The village of Kaiserswerth, north of Düsseldorf, fell within the area ruled by King Friedrich Wilhelm III of Prussia, who, unhappy with the competing Lutheran and Reformed Churches, decreed that they be united in one church, the Prussian Union. Fliedner was a member of that church.

Fliedner's goal in establishing a Deaconess Institute was not to reconstruct a biblical model but to respond to the needs and misery around him. On a trip to London in 1832 he had met an English Quaker, Elizabeth Fry, whose work with prisoners inspired Fliedner's own Home for Magdalens, one of the first works of the deaconesses.

A certain anti-Catholic sentiment, not surprising in a Protestant congregation of less than 200 isolated in a largely Catholic area, entered in. If the Catholics had Sisters of Mercy to care for the poor and sick, why shouldn't the Protestants have something similar? Fliedner's deaconesses lived in a community and professed loyalty to that community, but they were not bound permanently and took no vows of celibacy. For this centrist stand, Catholics were said to look down on them and some Protestants worried that they were too much like nuns.

The early foundation at Kaiserswerth combined care for the ill, for Magdalens, and for women released from prison, all of which Fliedner considered appropriate tasks for "the tender feelings of woman and her fine feminine tact in the mitigating of human needs, particularly among her own sex." The community quickly became a model. Florence Nightingale trained first at the Deaconess Institute in Kaiserswerth and then with the Daughters of Charity in Paris. Elizabeth Fry visited Kaiserswerth before starting the first English nurses' training school in London. Other deaconess houses sprang up all over Germany and Europe; by 1849, Rev. W.A. Passavant had brought deaconesses to the United States to staff a hospital in Pittsburgh.

Today there are deaconesses or women deacons in a number of U.S. churches, including Lutherans, Methodists, Anglicans and Presbyterians, and in Canada, in the United Church. These deaconesses have followed different models. Some are close to being Protestant sisterhoods, living in community; others are congregational officials. Some are chosen or appointed; some have responded to the call within. Some are volunteers; some are professionals. Some may marry, some not. With all this variety, it is not surprising that these women understand the diaconate differently, and that as ordained ministry was opened to women in these churches some chose to remain in the diaconate and some chose to become pastors. Occasionally there were tensions.

Already in 1970, Jeanne Barnes, a student in Quincy, Illinois, was working toward opening up the office of deacon to Catholic Women. She ran an ad in the *National Catholic Reporter* asking like-minded women to contact her and discovered that her aspirations were shared by many other women around the country.

This means that in all three branches of Christianity—Catholicism, Orthodoxy and Protestantism—the role of women in the diaconate is being discussed and evaluated.

In April of 1989, a Symposium on the History of Effects of the Diaconate met in Fribourg, Switzerland. "There was a major emphasis on women in the diaconate," according to Deacon Constantino J. Ferriola, Jr., the Executive Director of the U. S. Bishops' Committee on the Permanent Diaconate. Catholics from around the world reported on the diaconate in their own countries, and they were joined by deaconesses from the Church of England and from the Lutheran Church in this country. "Experiencing these women from other churches gave Catholics a very positive sense of the role of women deacons," Ferriola said.

Women and the diaconate would seem to be a good topic for interfaith dialogue today.

15

The Re-Introduction of the Permanent Diaconate

Most Reverend Ernest L. Unterkoefler, Bishop of Charleston, interviewed by Arlene Swidler on March 28, 1989:

Q. *Was there any talk about the permanent diaconate in this country before Vatican II?*

A. There was a small amount of discussion. Pope Pius XII gave it some impetus at the significant meeting in Assisi in the 1950s. In 1955 I became interested in the little paragraph about the permanent diaconate in the Assisi papers. Pope Pius XII was really the person who gave the idea of the permanent diaconate a bit of a push at that time.

Q. *Could you tell us about your experience at Vatican II in regard to discussion of the permanent diaconate?*

A. It is a very lengthy topic, but I will give a brief recounting. The subject of the possibility of the permanent diaconate was very favorably received when it was placed on the agenda. A number of questions were posed concerning how it would work and other related matters. There *were* opponents. Even from the United States there were some people who said that we should have acolytes and catechists, but not permanent deacons. Cardinal Ottaviani was against the diaconate, wanting laymen to be acolytes, not permanent deacons. Several others also were opposed. There was some opposition in the Third World. Africa has been a little slow on the diaconate and still has the system of acolytes and catechists.

Several questions on the permanent diaconate were presented to us for a vote. We voted with magnetic pencils, with the ballots being run through a machine. The vote could be obtained in a short time; 2500 votes could be processed in less than 30 minutes. The mechanical part of the voting process was very scientific.

It came out clearly at that time that there would be much discussion about celibacy and also the age factor for permanent deacons. We did not want the call to the permanent diaconate to get to the seminaries and draw seminarians away from celibacy. It was very clear in the Council, with many discussions by the Bishops, that whenever celibacy came up in the voting there was a tremendous vote from the Bishops of the world to preserve the celibate state.

Interest in the permanent diaconate moved along. I gave a talk at the United States Bishops' meeting in the North American College. An eminent Cardinal and many others did not think the concept was worthwhile, and I received only 17 votes in favor of my going before the Council to make an intervention. I didn't deliver the intervention verbally before the Council. I thought the majority of the Bishops from the United States were against it, and I didn't want to embarrass the majority. I sent my intervention in writing, which was equally as good. From that point on, there were probably fewer than 400 votes against the permanent diaconate in the final vote.

Then Pope Paul VI appointed me to a Commission, as a Bishop of the United States, with 12 other Bishops from around the world, to work on the elements of his *Motu Proprio,* which he was to put into effect in mid-summer, 1967. I went to the meeting in February. I was called to Rome quietly by Pope Paul VI, and we had a good talk on the permanent diaconate. He said, "You know, instead of having Bishops, Archbishops and Cardinals in the Curia, we could have permanent deacons. These men could be out in pastoral duty."

Q. *So then you were appointed to the position of Director of the Permanent Diaconate here because already during Vatican II you were seen as a leading proponent?*

A. Cardinal Dearden appointed me and told me to establish a Committee to evaluate the situation in the United States. We did this. We studied it very carefully, to see if it was feasible in the United States. It was not a great scientific survey. We were assessing the feelings on this matter in different areas.

As a result of our study, we came to the conclusion that the permanent diaconate would be viable in the United States. I drafted a request to Cardinal Cicognani, in the Secretariat of State, to authorize the National Conference of Catholic Bishops, which was already in existence, to inaugurate the permanent diaconate. Within four or five weeks we got the authorization, with no problems.

Q. *During this early period, during Vatican II and the beginning of the reestablishment here, was there any talk at all about women being included in the diaconate?*

A. There was no idea at all in the Council or in the preliminary discussions in the Commission preparing for the *Motu Proprio.* The idea of women in the diaconate came up for the first time when we were preparing guidelines. When we were preparing our first book of guidelines, which came out in 1970, we discussed women in the diaconate in the United States only. In the appendix of that guideline book you will see that we supported the diaconate for women. It is a brief statement, but we thought that this would be a very feasible thing for women's ministry; however, as the years went on, we met a lot of opposition from women who wanted to be priests and bishops. I backed off and never really got serious about women in the diaconate because we were getting very little support from women themselves about this.

Q. *During this early time, while the diaconate was being reestablished, how was the role of the deacon perceived? Was there a diversity of opinions and even a diversity in the way the deacons were working?*

A. It was an uncharted course, and we went rather carefully trying to figure out how this should work. We had a basic structure that came from the *Motu Proprio* and also from the Council. The deacon should emphasize the Word of God, he should emphasize sacramental ministry, and he should emphasize, perhaps more than anyone else in the Church, the social ministry of the Church, which we put under the canopy of charity. The committee was very intense on getting the deacons into the social ministry of the Church, which meant social justice, being the witness for all the problems that were going on at the time: the racial problems, the difficulties in Vietnam. We thought that the deacons could have a tremendous influence in social justice and particularly the entire social ministry, including taking up work with prisoners, immigrants, migrant workers and refugees. We had a great vision of the ministry of the deacon, and that vision is in motion fairly well right now.

Q. *Two questions here. First of all, I understand that several European National Conferences of Bishops have at one time or another petitioned Rome that women be included in the diaconate, and I wonder whether such a move has ever been considered here. Secondly, I have heard that at least an informal petition was sent in the case of Josephine Massyngberde Ford.*

A. Yes, I am familiar with Josephine's petition, which was refused; however, it was not *categorically* refused. It seemed to me that they were leaving the door open for further study. We have had personal representations before the Congregations about this, particularly during the 1970s. One of the heads of the Congregation on the Sacraments said that he could see the possibility of an Order of Deaconesses, not calling the women deacons but deaconesses.

Agnes Cunningham, a theologian, has given us a great deal of insight into this matter. She did a lot of study on the diaconate in the early Church. My conclusions about the diaconate in the early Church, in the first and second centuries particularly, are that women did perform diaconal functions. They performed, in particular, the Baptismal Rite, and this was very reasonable, very practical and very pastoral. These women instructed the new convert women. In those days, immersion was the way of baptism. The women would take the convert women to the river or creek and baptize them, as part of the liturgy. The bishop was seated and the women who performed the baptism would have a place at the side of the bishop during the liturgy. We are not clear, however, on the nature of the authorization of these women. It has not been determined in a definite way if they were commissioned, mandated by the individual bishop, or ordained to the diaconate. As time goes on, I become less impressed by the evidence that they were ordained. I am confident that they were commissioned or mandated by the bishop to perform diaconal functions. Whether they really received the Order of Deacon is a question that remains to be resolved.

Q. *Do you sense that there would be strong support for women in the permanent diaconate today, and do you see any change from the past?*

A. My sensitivity is that women who are interested in this matter would prefer to skip the permanent diaconate and to get to the priesthood and the episcopate. I became less enthusiastic about permanent deacons being women when some of the people interested in ordination said this was not really what they wanted. I would have thought that they might consider this a first step. I do not agree with the thinking, but some people considered the permanent diaconate for men as the first step to a married clergy. There is emphasis today, among people who promote women for the priesthood and episcopate, to continue to work in that direction. I see very little interest in and very little support for women in the permanent diaconate, and this observation is based on almost 28 years as a bishop.

If the diaconate for women did occur, it would take a lot of time for people to get used to the idea, just as it did with the permanent diaconate for men. That is why the Second Vatican Council, with all its wonderful principles and direction, is not in total operation yet. We have learned that any big movements in the Church take time. People are not ready for change. You have to nurture them and guide them. You can't make significant changes and electrify people overnight.

This is true in non-Catholic Churches. I have talked to many women who are ordained ministers. They have a difficult time in getting first-class appointments, because the people will not call them to ministry. You know that they have to be called by the congregation. In many areas, particularly in the South, the congregations will not call them. This has been very trying, and some of the women ministers have been defeated by attitudes and have given up their ministry. I don't want Catholic women to go through this with the permanent diaconate. We have had some difficulties with our congregations accepting our permanent deacons, but we have worked hard to get erroneous ideas and attitudes out of the Church.

Q. *Do you think perhaps some of the attitudes on the part of women are the result of a misunderstanding of the permanent diaconate? That this should not be seen by women as a step towards the priesthood, but as a different sort of ministry? Are women still thinking in pre-Vatican II terms?*

A. Yes, I think there is some misunderstanding, and that there is some pre-Vatican II thinking on the part of some women. We need broader vision to see how we are going to get women into ministry, and what ministries are open to women. I am confident that we would have much more success with the permanent diaconate or permanent deaconesses in the Church if there was not always the question of ordination to the priesthood and the episcopate.

Our experience with the permanent diaconate is that an infinitesimal percentage of these men want to become priests. They have no idea of becoming priests. They understand that their ministry is different from the priests' ministry, altogether different. It has another dimension, and through experience they are learning this. It may look as though they are doing some things like a priest, like distributing Communion, and sacramentally there may be some resemblances; but their total ministry is altogether different. This is a blessing, because today the diaconate in the Church is better understood in the United States than it ever has been in its history.

Q. *If the question was brought up today to the American Bishops, how many, do you think, would be in favor of women in the permanent diaconate?*

A. I have no idea whatsoever. I can say this: there is much more openness on the part of many bishops today to the idea of women in ministry. How they would handle a vote on the permanent diaconate for women, however, I don't know. I can sense the openness to greater ministries for women in discussions we have had on the Pastoral Letter on Women in Church and Society.

We keep trying to get ministries open, particularly acolytes, readers and lectors. Some women are not satisfied with that, but we have to start somewhere. Anyone who is familiar with the Church before Vatican II knows that men had to take those steps—lector and acolyte—to get to diaconate.

Bishops of today are much more open to a broader ministry for women than they would have been years ago. We see this in the Church, with what is permissible: women lectors, women Eucharistic ministers, and women in leadership. We have a woman as chairperson of our Ecumenical Commission, a woman Chancellor, a woman in charge of an entire social and human development program, and we have a Vicaress for Religious. She is the Vicaress for both men and women religious.

Q. *Would you say, though, that women who are serving as parish administrators and as hospital chaplains are, in a sense, functioning as deacons?*

A. We can say that they are performing diaconal functions. I would phrase it in this way: they are performing certain diaconal functions without a commission in the sense of the diaconate. They are commissioned, they are mandated, and they are recognized, but the total diaconal life is not theirs. Piece by piece, they are receiving diaconal work.

Q. *Do you have any other ideas, insights or memories that you would like to add?*

A. I have a lot of memories. I think the permanent diaconate for men in the United States is going along fairly well. Even after some development of the diaconate, however, I had several Cardinals and some prelates in Washington tell me that this movement needed to slow down, that it was going too fast, and that too many mistakes had been made. I kept insisting, even to Apostolic Delegates, that we cannot frustrate the work of the Holy Spirit. If almost 10,000 men have come to be ordained in the permanent diaconate, this is the work of God. The whole program could have collapsed before it got underway. If, across the nation, only ten men had come forward, that would have been the end of the permanent diaconate program. Somehow or other, the enthusiasm and the momentum were in the air and the men came forward in large numbers. They are still coming forward, although not in such large numbers.

Almost 10,000 vocations in a period of about 15 years is a tremendous benefit to the Church. I am not in any way trying to compare the deacon with the priest, but I would say that we would have been most fortunate if 10,000 priests had been ordained in the last ten years. This did not occur.

Many years ago, there were efforts in some dioceses to be overly cautious in admitting candidates for priestly formation. I remember this well, as I served in several Chancery offices. Men were denied admittance to priestly formation programs because they did not have a B average in their academic work or because they had not studied Latin. In one of the Chanceries in which I worked, some years before I came here to serve, a man applied for acceptance as a seminarian for that diocese. He was denied because it was felt that he had an insufficient background in Latin, even though the man had a pharmacy degree. He was accepted for priestly formation elsewhere and became the Superior General of a religious order.

There was an effort to be too stringent in the admittance requirements for permanent deacons, also, but I exhorted other bishops to let the men come forward. Surely there have been mistakes. This is human nature. Some of the deacons did not live up to what they said they were going to do, but these men have been a very small percentage of the permanent deacons. We have troubles in the priesthood, at times, and we have troubles with all segments of society, at times.

The diaconate of the Diocese of Charleston has worked out rather well. We have over 30 deacons and about 30 to 40 men in training. The candidates go through a four-year program. We have had setbacks with a few of our men, but the overall program has been very beneficial. For instance, Charleston is a port city, and is the second largest port on the East Coast. It is a container port. Actually there are four port locations here, with four different docks: Charleston, North Charleston, the Wando in Mt. Pleasant and the port in Georgetown, South Carolina. If I did not have a permanent deacon to do the work of port ministry, I don't know how the port personnel would be served. I have no priest available to be assigned to this maritime ministry. Our permanent deacon, however, is at the docks for six or seven hours a day, taking care of people coming in on French ships, German ships, English ships, ships from South America and many other countries. Many of these people are Catholics. Our deacon sees that these people get to church, he brings them rosaries, Bibles, prayer books and other religious articles, and he assists them in making long-distance phone calls. He does not have to be a priest to direct and to aid the maritime personnel.

We have women, mostly members of religious orders, performing diaconal functions, such as prison ministry. There are five or six religious women working in the prisons. Some Sisters have been there for as many as 15 years, educating the prisoners, getting them socialized for their acceptance back into society, and guiding their spiritual destinies. One of our Sisters travels all over South Carolina, covering small areas where there are no large groups together in prisons. We have women in youth ministry in our prisons. One Sister deals primarily with youthful violators. So apostolates such as port ministry and prison ministry, excellent examples of diaconal functions, have developed for men and for women. An especially significant aspect about the permanent diaconate program in South Carolina is that we have attracted black men to this ministry.

Q. *Of the almost 10,000 deacons, 93 or 94 percent are married. About half of the wives have gone through the training. Some of these 4500 women, understanding well what the diaconate entails, might be interested in the diaconate themselves.*

A. Right from the beginning, we insisted that wives go through the training along with their husbands. That was one of our cardinal points in the permanent diaconate program. Even the children, we insisted, should get some benefits from the training. We don't want a husband and father to come home and say, "I'm different now." We want his wife and his children, if they are old enough, to get into some of the instructional program, but we *insist* that the wives must come to everything.

I think that these wives would understand the diaconate better than those who have not had that intimate experience with the ministry of their husband, and some of these wives might be interested in assuming diaconal roles. It could be a detriment to the family, however, if a father *and* a mother devoted many hours during the week to diaconal functions. Their family is their vocation also, and we must always preserve the unity and sanctity of family life. Even if their parents had a team ministry and worked together, following the same schedule, there would be the possibility that their children might feel neglected. We endeavor always to foster and to strengthen the bonds of family life. At some future time, if both a husband and wife desired diaconal ministry, I am sure adjustments, compromises and solutions could be achieved.

16

The Permanent Diaconate in Today's Church

Deacon Samuel Taub

The Experience of the First Generation of the Restored Diaconate in the United States

Equally important is the contribution that a married deacon makes to the transformation of family life. He and his wife, having entered into a communion of life, are called to help and serve each other. So intimate is their partnership and unity in the sacrament of marriage that the church fittingly requires the wife's consent before her husband can be ordained a permanent deacon (Can. 1031 §2).

As the current guidelines for the permanent diaconate point out, the nurturing and deepening of mutual, sacrificial love between husband and wife constitute perhaps the most significant involvement of a deacon's wife in her husband's public ministry in the Church. Today, especially, this is no small service.

In particular, the deacon and his wife must be a living example of fidelity and indissolubility in Christian marriage before a world which is in dire need of such signs. By facing in a spirit of faith the challenges of married life and the demands of daily living, they strengthen the family life not only of the Church community but of the whole society. They also show how the obligations of family, work and ministry can be harmonized in the service of the Church's mission. Deacons and their wives and children can be a great encouragement to all others who are working to promote family life.

Pope John Paul II

In these words, addressed to deacons and their wives in his visit to Detroit in 1987, the Holy Father not only affirmed the deacons and wives of deacons in our country but reflected accurately the primary relationship of woman to the diaconate which has developed over the course of the past twenty years. Twenty years is perhaps but a moment of time in the long life of the Church. But it marks the history of the diaconate in the United States and the relationships of this life-long commitment of service to the Church as a growing and developing expression of *diakonia*.

In 1971, the bishops of our country published their guidelines for the formation and ministry of permanent deacons; in this document the bishops envisioned the deacon, married or unmarried, as a living sacrament of service. It was already clear in the two years following the initiation of diocesan formation programs that the majority of men who presented themselves for a lifetime of service to the Church in the order of deacon were married and fathers of children. Taking this into account, twelve of the 182 guidelines in the 1971 document were devoted to the wife and children of the deacon during the formation and post-ordination years.

Two guidelines should be especially noted here because they directly influenced the manner in which the diaconate was introduced in its formative years.

> 127. Most deacon training programs take the candidate away from his wife and family two evenings a week; periodic weekend retreats or special meetings add to this time away; and the candidate spends additional time with the church or civic community of which he is a part. Aside from the question of time, the nature of a deacon's commitment to the community has reverberations in his family. Though the time he can give is limited and his commitment to his wife and family has clear priority, there is a new kind

of belonging to the community that has to be carefully considered throughout the formation so that the accepting of ordination becomes a free and conscious choice, shared and supported by the man's wife and children.

As envisioned above, in the beginning wives of candidates had little or no part in formation classes. This began to change slowly. By 1976, not only was participation of wives of candidates being strongly encouraged, but in several dioceses it was being required. This factor became increasingly important as deacon with wife reflected ever more seriously on their first life-long commitment to each other in the sacrament of marriage. We hold that in the sacramental marriage, the two spouses become one. In what way then does the wife enter into the diaconate of her husband?

The guideline cited above also established another clear principle which has endured. First priority in the life of a married deacon (and 94% of the nearly 9,000 deacons in the United States are married) must be his wife and family. A second priority was assigned to the deacon's job or profession by which he supported himself and his family. The third priority in his life was to be his ministry.

The first four permanent deacon programs were launched four years after the end of the Second Vatican Ecumenical Council. It is sometimes difficult to recall the excitement, the expectations, the unlimited possibilities of expanding the experience of Church which characterized those times. Some of this is reflected in the "Epilogue" of the 1971 guidelines, titled "New Directions," which focuses on the minimum age for ordination of permanent deacons (the bishops set 35 years as the minimum age), celibacy as it relates to the permanent deacon, and the ordination of women to the diaconate.

> 168. The third critical question concerns the ordination of women as deacons. Many women, lay and religious, have offered to serve in the ordained ministry and question the justice of being excluded. Among deacon candidates themselves and leaders of training programs, there is a growing conviction that women would strengthen the diaconal ministry.

169. The Bishops' Committee has spent many hours of discussion on all three of these questions, listening to people who sincerely seek a change in church law in order that the gospel message and the clarity of Christ might be communicated more effectively. After the widely circulated February, 1971 report of the Catholic Theological Society of America had offered strong arguments in favor of ordination of women, the Bishops' Committee discussed the question with individuals and groups who expressed reactions for or against. The committee of bishops has continued to pursue all three questions by listening to what people in the apostolate are saying and by carrying that message to churches in other countries and the Holy See.

The matter of ordination of women to the diaconate has remained on the agenda of the Bishops' Committee on the Permanent Diaconate with varying degrees of priority, depending on the needs of the time. By direct contact with the International Centre for the Diaconate in Freiburg, West Germany (through the United States Executive Director, who is a member of the Centre's Executive Board), the members of the Committee have kept abreast of developments in Europe, especially through an exchange of papers and studies on the possibilities of the ordination of women to the diaconate.

Experience of the Diaconate in the First Decade of the Renewal 1968-1978

During this first decade there was a dramatic growth in the permanent diaconate as deacon formation programs were established in 114 dioceses and the number of deacons grew to nearly four thousand.

With this growth came a developing appreciation of the need for the participation of the wife of the deacon candidate in the formation of her husband. Such participation deepened the wife's understanding of the mission of the Church, her gifts and the opportunity to exercise them on behalf of the Church either individually or in partnership with her deacon husband.

Not all wives of deacon candidates were able to take part fully in a formation program. This was especially true of wives who were working outside the home, either full or part time, and those who were still raising young children at home. It was becoming clear, however, as married deacons became more numerous, that the wife who was involved in the formation program and later shared in her husband's ministry was less likely to feel stress and more likely to express satisfaction with her husband's participation in the ministry as a member of the clergy.

These conclusions were authenticated by the results of a four-phased national study of the permanent diaconate in our country, the first of its kind, which was undertaken by the Bishops' Committee on the Permanent Diaconate in 1978 and published in 1981.

In these first years of diaconal renewal women other than wives of candidates were invited to take a full and active part in several diocesan deacon formation programs. When this fact was referred to the Bishops' Committee on the Permanent Diaconate for comment or approval, members of the Committee would point out the inappropriateness, inasmuch as no woman could be ordained a deacon.

In these several dioceses, headed by bishops who perceived that Rome was moving toward allowing women to be ordained deacons, both men and women were admitted to a diocesan formation program. In one diocese there were upward of 75 persons in such a program. When it became obvious the ordination of women would not be in the foreseeable future, the programs were disbanded and no one was ordained a permanent deacon. It was the judgment of one bishop that to ordain the men and not the women would not be fair.

During 1976 and 1977, the Bishops' Committee on the Permanent Diaconate showed a heightened interest in the participation of women in ministry and in pursuing the ordination question on a deeper theological level.

In February of 1976, at one of two general sessions of the fourth annual meeting of the diocesan directors of the permanent deacons, papers by Agnes Cunningham, S.S.C.M., and John Sheets, S.J., devoted to the theme of "Women in the Ministry" and the question of ordination of women stimulated wider interest in the ordination question. In September of 1977 the Administrative Committee of the National Conference mandated that the Bishops' Committee on the Permanent Diaconate in collaboration with the Doctrine Committee initiate theological studies on the question of diaconal functions historically undertaken by women. At its 1977 meeting in Louisville, the National Federation of Priests' Councils resolved to petition the Sacred Congregation for the Doctrine of Faith for such actions as necessary to open the permanent diaconate to all baptized persons in the Roman Catholic Church.

Although these projects were pursued by the member of the Bishops' Committee on the Permanent Diaconate, they have not been brought to resolution. The most recent contribution to the literature as a result of the Committee's initiative was a 1983 report by Sister Agnes Cunningham, S.S.C.M., and Reverend John Sheets, S.J., titled "Diaconal Functions Historically Undertaken by Women." And there the matter rests. In all other respects, the diaconate continued to grow, not only in numbers but in the variety of ministries in which deacons have been engaged.

The Second Decade of Diaconate Renewal 1979-1989

As experience of the diaconate accumulated, a number of adjustments were made in diocesan formation programs.

Formation was extended by one or two years. The average is now four years. A greater balance has been achieved between academic (theological) and pastoral formation with an accompanying understanding of how spiritual formation binds all the rest. Bishops have increasingly demanded high standards for deacons who exercise the charism of public proclamation, and this is reflected in increased proportion of time allocated to homiletics, Scripture and theology.

Deacons are perceived as having their greatest potential in the ministry of charity, as discerners of needs in the marketplace, as a bridge between the secular and the spiritual. The deacon is implanted in the secular world, yet marked with the character of orders which impels him to connect the secular with the world of faith. Deacons have been especially effective through informal discussions in the market place, better exploring an understanding of the Faith as they become recognized as a sacramental sign of presence of Jesus—Servant.

Deacons add a new sense of witness, broaden the understanding of ministry, and enhance a spirit of solidarity within the Church. They provide a possibility for an enhancement of team ministry on the parish level in meeting the daily needs of the parishioners, stimulating more lay participation in ministry. Lay persons see a man from that parish, one like themselves, dedicate himself more deeply to the service of God, with the recognition and mandate of the Church, meanwhile integrating the responsibilities of marriage and secular employment as an example for others to follow. As the love relationship in marriage is enriched by ministry, so marriage and family serve as a springboard for the deacon's service to the wider community. In the minority community a deacon, coming from the midst of the community, heightens the sense of belonging to Church because the Church has tapped indigenous ministerial leadership.

Almost parallel with the renewal of the diaconate had been the proliferation of lay ministers, both professional and volunteer. During this time the Diocese of Toledo first experimented in a structured way with the development of programs of formation for lay ministers and the integration of deacon and lay ministry formation. Within several years at least twelve other dioceses initiated similar programs. In such programs two years of formation were shared by candidates for lay ministry and with prospective candidates for the diaconate.

Initially the bishops of the Committee on the diaconate had reservations about this development. After approximately five years, the Committee's secretariat completed a study citing both the positive and negative experiences of each integrated diocesan program. After weighing the evidence, members of the Committee endorsed the continuation of such programs, understanding that "integration" was something of a misnomer. Actually, lay ministry formation became a pre-requisite for a man who wished to be considered as a candidate for the diaconate. The positive aspect of such an "integrated" program was that future deacons would have shared two years of formation with those lay ministers with whom they would be engaged in ministry. They would have shared prayer, study and pastoral practicum, surely an advantage in realizing how each exercised charisms which contribute to the development of a communion of ministries.

The 1984 revision of the bishops' guidelines for the formation and ministry of permanent deacons (No. 121) states: "Deacons and priests should have a genuine respect for each other and for the integrity of the two distinct ministries. For the good of the church, the two ministries must be exercised in communion with one another." This is the ideal toward which priests and deacons are working amidst some tensions. That tensions would arise perhaps was inevitable especially considering the differences in lifestyle and ministerial formation. The restoration of the diaconate was but one among many reforms that were undertaken in the post-conciliar years. What is encouraging is the effort of all who are engaged in this communion of ministries to discern ministerial charisms and the manner in which they may be exercised in responding to the overwhelming human needs.

And now, what of the future?

The Ministry of the Second Generation of Deacons 1990-2000

As a premise, I believe that it is necessary to understand that the second generation of deacons will have come out of an experience of the Church entirely different from that of the first generation. Those who are formed for and ordained permanent deacons truly will be children of the Second Vatican Ecumenical Council. The experience of relationships with bishops, priests, religious (especially women religious), and lay ministers will have been quite different from those of the generation which preceded them. Their experience of Church and their whole notion of who they are as Church, the exercise of charisms in the service of the Church, the communion of ministries which have been called into being to serve the servant Church will have a decided influence on the formation of future deacons.

In the decade ahead we can expect that those who are currently identified as "minority" increasingly will assume an ownership of Church, looking forward to the time in the not too distant future when they will constitute the majority. Those who have been responsible for the development of the diaconate have been recruiting in the minority communities from the very beginning of the renewal of this servant ministry. As a result there are today over one thousand Hispanic deacons ministering in their communities. And we can expect their numbers to increase in the decade ahead.

Among the first generation it became common for the wife of a deacon candidate to take a full part in the formation of her husband. Following this experience, many wives shared in the ministry of their deacon husbands. But as wives take on outside jobs in the majority of marriages in the Catholic community, their ability to take part in a formation program will become seriously curtailed. This will surely have an impact on the marriages of younger deacons. It will be the responsibility of those charged with the formation of deacons to take this into account in revising programs of spiritual formation and post-ordination continuing formation.

Based on the conviction that the renewal of the permanent diaconate is a response to the working of the Holy Spirit, we should anticipate the continued growth of the diaconate. The increased effectiveness of this ministry will be based on a continued refinement of the criteria for the selection of deacon candidates, the revision of a formation program which responds to the future needs for deacon ministry, and increasingly effective in pastoring of deacons by diocesan bishops who in their own guidelines have asserted their responsibility for the post-ordination care—spiritual, academic, pastoral—of their deacons.

Saved for the last is a final comment on the possibility of the ordination of women to diaconate. Although it is abundantly clear that for the immediate future there is no likelihood that the present discipline of the Church will change, it is certain that successive Committees on the Permanent Diaconate will be the primary agent within the National Conference of Catholic Bishops to stimulate and promote the necessary theological studies which will be required before this question is once again placed before the competent dicasteries of the Holy See.

17

De Vocatione et Missione Liacorum in Ecclesia Syro-Malabarese

Address to the 1987 Synod of Bishops
Bishop Kuriakose Kunnacherry of Kottayam

The centrality of the people of God in the life of the church is basic to the whole outlook of the Oriental churches. The Syro-Malabar church, rooted in the East Syrian ecclesial tradition, focuses attention on the holy people of God gathered around the risen Lord. So the *laos* or laity came in the first place, and hierarchy and clergy were rightly considered the leaders and ministers called to serve the people. The predominance of the laity came on account of several historical reasons. First of all, the East Syrian Church from its Edessan origins was deeply influenced by the example of the Essenian and Qumran communities, and the early Christians of this church considered baptism as an entry into a covenanted life of constant vigilance. It felt itself as a community of grace, with every member having a share in the sanctifying role of the church.

There was a wide involvement of the whole church, both men and women, in the celebration of the sacraments. This is particularly evident by the role of *msamsanitha* or deaconess, who was specially ordained to help in the administration of baptism to women, to distribute holy communion under special circumstances and form, etc. Even today, the ordination service of bishops in some Oriental rites contains words explicitly conferring power to ordain deaconesses. This power was conferred on me when I was ordained bishop. But so far I have not used this power. It is felt that the tradition of admitting women to the diaconate did not survive the era of early Christianity. But there are evidences that suggest the ordination of deaconesses in the Oriental churches (Maronite, Greek Orthodox) as late as the 18th century.

Deaconesses can play a liturgical, sacramental, catechetical and prophetical role in the church. The ministry of women in the church would be a new kind of ministry. This will have patterns and forms of ministry proper to itself. Women would bring a different quality to certain ministries in the church. This is especially true regarding teaching ministry in schools and healing ministry in hospitals.

In the present day context of the church, selected, educated, and mature Catholic women, both lay and religious, can be of immense help in the apostolate. The restoration of the institution of the deaconess will be a positive contribution of the church in upholding the dignity of women and in affirming their equality with men in holding responsible positions in the church. Besides, it will be an effective way to remedy the shortage of priests in many countries and to open a new field in the pastoral ministry with the maternal touch of Mother Church. It will also satisfy to a certain extent the aspirations of the women who clamor even for priesthood.

The Eucharist was the communitarian service of the whole people. It began with the celebration of the word in the middle of the church, the people standing around the bishop and clergy. Throughout the Divine Liturgy appeared as one celebration of the people led by the bishop.

There was an intimate relationship between people and their priests. No one could be accepted for priestly ministry without the consent of *Palliyogam* or parish council. Priestly formation itself was not merely a training for ministry, but an ongoing interaction between people and those selected to lead them. Sacred functions, including the Divine Liturgy, began with the celebrant formally asking the permission of the people.

What the Church needs today is an active involvement of the laity in all aspects of ecclesial life. The pilgrim people of God has to realize together its mission in the world to transform it into God's Kingdom. In this process, persons are more important than territory and institutions, and consequently human rights and cultural values of the laity have to be respected.

For Further Reading

Bishops' Committee on the Permanent Diaconate, *A National Study of the Permanent Diaconate in the United States.* Washington, D.C.: United States Catholic Conference Publications Office, 1981. Includes both a history and an analysis of the Permanent Deacon Study.

Bishops' Committee on the Permanent Diaconate, *Permanent Deacons in the United States, Guidelines for Their Formation and Ministry.* Washington, D.C.: United States Catholic Conference Publications Office, 1971. Provides a good general discussion of the permanent diaconate and the spiritual formation of the deacon. Suggestions for changes in the diaconate for the future are also discussed.

"Deaconess," in *Schaff-Herzog Encyclopedia of Religious Knowledge.* New York: Funk and Wagnall, 1909 and later reprints. Seven large pages of historical treatment, especially useful for its discussion of the deaconesses in the various Protestant churches in the nineteenth century.

FitzGerald, Kyriaki Karidoyanes, "The Characteristics and Nature of the Order of the Deaconess," in Thomas Hopko, *Women and the Priesthood.* New York: St. Vladimir's Seminary Press, 1983. A good summary of women in the diaconate in Eastern Orthodox Churches up until the present day.

Gryson, Roger, *The Ministry of Women in the Early Church.* Collegeville, Minn.: The Liturgical Press, 1976. A careful analysis of the textual sources on women's roles in the early Church.

McKenna, Sister Mary Lawrence, S.C.M.M., *Women of the Church: Role and Renewal.* New York: P. J. Kenedy & Sons, 1967. A clear presentation of the various roles women played in the early centuries of the Church.